Becoming Dianne

Becoming Dianne

DIANNE KELLY

Healing House
PUBLISHING

First Published in Australia in 2025
by Healing House Publishing
www.healinghousepublishing.com

© Dianne Kelly

All rights reserved. No part of this publication may be reproduced, stored in a retrieval system, or transmitted, in any form or by any means, electronic, mechanical, photocopying, recording, or otherwise, without the prior written permission of the publisher.

The National Library of Australia Cataloguing-in-Publication entry

Title: Becoming Dianne
Author: Dianne Kelly
Paperback ISBN: 978-1-7641185-1-4
Editor: Vanessa Barrington
Cover and Internal Design: Heidi Glasson

Healing House Publishing is committed to publishing works of quality and integrity. In that spirit, we are proud to offer this book to our readers; however, the story, the experiences, and the words are the author's alone.

Foreword

It is an honour to write a foreword for Dianne's book, which is truly a testament to Sir Winston Churchill's quote of "Never, never give up" from his 1941 speech on the importance of resilience and determination in the face of adversity.

Amazingly, though women in Australia were given the vote in 1902, it was not until 2008, only 17 years ago and over 100 years later, that single women like Dianne were legally able to have fertility treatment with donor gametes without a man's involvement.

As this book emphasises, and research following donor-conceived children from birth to adulthood has shown, it is love and truth that matter most to children born through third-party origins, i.e. donor origins. The presence of a father, or two parents, or any genetic connection is not essential for children to thrive. The quality of the family relationships

FOREWORD

and support of the surrounding community is what matters. So, Dianne's book showing the love, caring and support of those around her through her fertility journey should be an encouragement to other women wishing to follow her path.

I hope this book inspires you.

Dr Anne Clark
MPS, MBChB, RCOG, RANZCOG, CREI, APP
Founder and Medical Director of Fertility First

BECOMING DIANNE

> *"There is no greater agony than bearing an untold story inside you."*
>
> – MAYA ANGELOU

Before I even began my IVF journey, I already knew your name. My precious "E," the love I have for you is beyond measure, and with each passing day, it grows stronger, more profound. Soon, we will meet on this earth, and I will finally experience the joy of holding you close. Until then, my heart swells with anticipation, knowing that this love will only deepen as we begin this new chapter together.

This journey would not have been the same without the guidance and inspiration of a remarkable woman—my mentor, Tonya Leigh. Through her wisdom and insight, I've learned so much about myself, life, and the art of chasing my desires with grace, elegance, and courage. Tonya, you are my hero and my inspiration, and I cannot thank you enough for introducing me to transformative work that has shaped my life in ways I never imagined.

Disclaimer

The information provided in this book is for general informational purposes only and is not intended as medical advice, diagnosis, or treatment. I am not a medical professional, and the content shared here is based on personal experience, research, or opinion.

Readers should always consult with a qualified healthcare provider or medical professional regarding any questions or concerns they may have about their health or a medical condition. Never disregard professional medical advice or delay seeking it because of something you have read in this book.

Author's Note

This memoir reflects my own memories, thoughts, and emotions as truthfully as I can share them. Out of respect for the privacy of others, I've changed some names and identifying details. While the stories are real, certain people may recognise themselves or events differently—that's the nature of memory. This is my version, told from where I stood.

Contents

Chapter 1: Childhood, relationships and career	15
Chapter 2: Relationships	94
Chapter 3: Road to motherhood	103
Chapter 4: Letting go of my path	135
Chapter 5: Discovering SOSI and my truest self	170
Chapter 6: Donor cycles	181
Chapter 7: Pregnancy	197
Chapter 8: Birth and motherhood	209
Acknowledgements	239
Recommended Resources	241
Glossary	242
References	243

INTRODUCTION

Introduction

I'm Dianne, 50 years young and proud mum to two-year-old Eva, as I write this book; my miracle baby girl, who was six years in the making. I made a conscious choice to be a single mum in my late 40s, using egg and sperm donors to conceive my precious baby girl.

Becoming Dianne is a story about love, fully embracing desires, life's challenges, frustrations and facing fears. Mostly it's about embodying my 2024 word of the year, COURAGE.

It's my story and mine alone; childhood memories, career, personal and romantic relationships, and how these influenced my journey to motherhood. Never expecting life to turn out as it has, and the path taken to get here, I am incredibly grateful for all that I have and have learnt along the way. The path to and of IVF is a deeply personal one, and this book is in no way designed to say that my way will work for others, or that others' paths are any better or less than mine. We each have our own individual journey through life and make the best decisions with the knowledge we have at the time.

My hope for you, as you read my story, is that you feel less alone, inspired to build a deeper connection with yourself, and desire to live your life to the fullest. Embrace the lessons in this book, and you'll change the trajectory of your life (no matter what you desire). The benefit of hindsight is a wonderful thing and better than regret, lack or a scarcity mindset. Learn from others, as well as from yourself; I promise you that you won't regret it. So, without further ado, in the words of my mentor Tonya Leigh:

Bring it - I was made for this!

*"Let your hopes, not your hurts,
shape your future"*

– ROBERT H. SCHULLER

CHAPTER 1

Childhood, Relationships & Career

"Every day begins with an act of courage and hope: getting out of bed"

– MASON COOLEY

CHILDHOOD, RELATIONSHIPS & CAREER

How my journey began

It was the start of 2024, and what an extraordinary year it was going to be! How did I know this? Not by some magical spell or oracle. I trusted myself and in what I could achieve with my life. Mind you, this was only a recent belief I developed following much heartache, loss, disappointment, disconnection from self, and living a robotic life up until three years prior. That was me in a nutshell, living full of hope and wishful thinking, and wondering why I wasn't living the life of my dreams. Until this point, I had lived with constant intrusive thoughts, such as:

"You're not good enough."
"It only happens to others, not you."
"You're too much."
"You're not skinny enough or tall enough or pretty enough."
"You're the 'make do' girl, not the future partner."

These thoughts crept in so constantly that most of the time I didn't even notice; it was such an ingrained habit. All I knew was that I felt sad, anxious, frustrated, and lost. The heaviness felt so overpowering at times that I would literally shut myself away from everyone and everything and have a good cry. I never wanted anyone to see me in this state as I was embarrassed about what they might think or say, so I saved my crying for the shower, where I felt safe, alone, warm and protected. Unsure specifically what I was crying about, but the tight knot in my stomach grew and grew until it would consume my entire body as though I was being suffocated by a snake ever so slowly coiling around me. My whole body felt tense, my neck stiff, my shoulders clenched. And no one said anything. The funny thing is, though, perhaps they never noticed, and on the outside, I never showed them. The disconnect between what I was feeling on the inside and how I showed up on the outside was greatly disjointed. I wanted people to read my mind, as if that were a real thing.

Most of my negative thoughts centred on relationships, both romantic and platonic. I always felt the odd one out wherever I was, like I just didn't fit in anywhere. This began during my high school years, and I could never put my finger on why. *Was I that unapproachable and unlikeable? Was it even real?*

Sitting on the outside and looking in on fun, love, joy and adventure, I watched others living what I so desperately longed for. I really found it hard to connect with anyone, including myself. Instead, I became who I thought I should be and who others said I needed to be in order to be loved, validated, and fit in. Wearing clothes I didn't always like or feel comfortable in, I tried smoking cigarettes because I thought it would make me 'cool', and said yes to everything and everyone, whether I really wanted to or not.

The problem was I still didn't fit in. I was the 'make do' girl; never the girlfriend. Every time I saw my crush with someone else, it only served to reinforce this belief and self-hatred. My heart would shatter into a million pieces every time, questioning what was so wrong with me and why I couldn't just fix it.

No matter how hard I tried, willing for things to work out, they didn't.

My daily routine (if you could call it one) couldn't have been more habitual if I tried. I got up, made the same cup of coffee (weak, white, with one sugar), ate the same breakfast (Weet-bix and strawberries, followed by peanut butter toast), wore the same baggy, unflattering clothes, and headed off to work. No intentionality, love or care behind any of it.

Over the decades, work played a significant part in my identity, again unconsciously so. The identities I held onto tightly included those of the hard worker, the fixer, and the people pleaser. Working long hours, doing the workload of two people and managing the more complex tasks were never enough. I wanted approval, validation and acknowledgement, and it never came. Not from me nor others. So I continued to do more and more and more. Still, the result was the same. Beyond exhausted mentally and emotionally, I continued to try. Call it blind determination, stubbornness or a desperate cry for love. I saw myself as a hard worker, one of the best in the company and was extremely proud of that. I felt validated in my work and self-assured in my ability, with not one inch of doubt creeping in.

Then comes love... unrequited love. This shattered my heart more than once into tiny pieces, and no matter what I did, who I became or how I dressed, the result was the same. Putting their needs, wants and interests before my own, not to mention not speaking up when I was belittled or disrespected. Instead, I cried into my pillow so no one could see my anguish, fearful of further belittling or worse, being ignored. I told myself, "Suck it up, Dianne, this is just how things are", wiping away the tears and getting on with things. Never speaking up, showing my hurt, or, God forbid, challenging them on what they said or did to me. Why, you ask?

It was plain and simple. I was scared they would leave me if I did, and that felt the absolute worst thing that could happen. It never occurred to me that it could actually have been a good thing for me to be out of such toxic relationships. The fear of being left felt so overwhelmingly traumatic for me, I allowed them to disrespect me. And ultimately, the thing I feared the most happened anyway: they left. I felt even worse then.

Life wasn't always so doom and gloom. I had the most loving grandparents. Each, in their way, showed me regularly how much they loved and were proud of me. They blessed me with hand-drawn cartoons, personalised poems, unique pottery and leather creations, all of which I still own and proudly display. No matter what, they believed in me.

Losing my maternal grandfather before I was 10 was beyond devastating. I truly loved him and miss him every day. Sitting in the church pew at his funeral, already feeling sad and in disbelief that he was really gone. Then hearing the Minister say, "and God called Edward up to join him in everlasting peace". Those words still sadden me. God took away the most beloved person in my life - who the heck did God think he was?

The power of someone's words knows no bounds, and at 50 years young, I am taken straight back to that little girl sitting at her Pop's funeral. Sadness gave rise to anger. Anger this God that I was supposed to believe in could be so cruel and heartless.

My grandmother's homes were a place of comfort, warmth, love and peace. Salivating at Nana's homemade bacon and egg pies or shortbread upon our arrival, we tasted the buttery texture and deliciousness with every bite. I swear I never tasted anything nearly as good as hers. The vanilla scent of her powder compact transports me to her warm embrace, soft, kind words, no matter how much of a ratbag I was to her. Seeing past the rough edges of my other Nana, who had to grow up too soon, yet was the protector that everyone went to when in need. Her rockmelon was the sweetest tasting, nothing quite like I've had before, until I discovered she had soaked it in sherry prior to us visiting. No wonder I slept on the car ride home. Still sweet memories of some amazing women.

My paternal grandfather, who wrote such heartfelt and personalised poetry when I was born and then again when I was accepted into university. His carrot cake was often delivered to me by Dad, with julienne carrot strips placed on top and wrapped in foil. He would always call, telling me that my special parcel was sealed, and if I opened it when Dad handed it to me, to call him back immediately. Carrot cake has not tasted the same since he passed over thirty years ago. Such sweet memories.

My Year 10 high school formal was marred by a badly dislocated knee, which left me wearing a full leg cast from my bottom to my ankle for six weeks, all while trying on formal dresses. The struggle was real, trust me. Imagine trying on a dress where you are unable to bend one leg and have to precariously balance on the other to climb into your dress of choice. Not the smartest move, but it did provide entertainment for many around me.

Blessed with the cast removed only a few weeks beforehand, I felt nervous and slightly weak on that leg, having not bent it for quite a long time. Heels were definitely not an option! More like a safety hazard. Filled with nervous excitement, I could hardly wait to see my crush, Beau. He was tall, dark and handsome - such a cliche. Beau and I had been exchanging notes in science class for a few months prior, and I had hoped desperately that he would ask me to be his date. He didn't. Still filled with hope and optimism, I walked into the school hall that night, scanning the room to see if I could spot him. I did; my heart skipped a beat. He looked so handsome. Chatting to his mates, he didn't notice me arriving. Sticking close to my girlfriends, I sank back into myself, hoping no one would see my embarrassment and shame. Others knew of our flirting, and thankfully said nothing to me. Dance music played, and I spent most of the night scanning to see where Beau was. I kept asking myself, why hadn't he asked me to dance yet? It was nearly time to go home.

The DJ announced the last song of the night, and my heart sank. Beau and I weren't going to have our first dance. We weren't going to have any dance. And then I turned around and saw him standing behind me. Beaming, I turned to face him, filled with nervousness and squealing with joy inside. He extended his hand and led me to the dance floor. We stood close to one another and swayed to the music. I felt my heart burst, and time stood still. I was lucky to have the last dance. He had picked me.

Now hold up a second, he left it to the last song to ask me to dance. Was I really the last option? I never thought about it that way at the time. I was floating on air then and all the way home that night. *But why did he leave me to last? And why was I ok with that?*

2023 was my best year yet by far. I welcomed in the start of 2023 six weeks pregnant and feeling a mixture of ecstasy, anxiety and fear. Scared of what my family would think of me being pregnant at 48, let alone choosing to be a single mum and using double donors to make it all happen. Anxious whether this time round the pregnancy would reach full term, or as had happened previously, I'd miscarry or have a chemical pregnancy. A chemical pregnancy is a very early miscarriage that happens before five weeks of pregnancy. It occurs when an embryo implants in the uterine lining but fails to develop. Both are emotionally devastating. Ecstasy, as this time round, I believed was my time. Bubs was going to stick, and my dream of motherhood would become a reality. Riding a rollercoaster of emotions, I kept the news to myself, fearing others' judgment, criticism, and possibly even worse: failing again.

While we (society) have come a long way in the world of IVF and understanding the varied ways to make up a family, there remains stigma around donor conception and, in particular, double donor conception. It isn't a topic many know about, let alone discuss openly. By sharing my story, I hope to raise awareness and acceptance of different ways of being, conceiving and family makeup.

So I sit here, thinking back to that time and what led me there, as well as where I am right now. Why did I wait until my 40s to try for a child? Why did I choose to be a single parent and choose double donor conception? For that, we need to backtrack six years…

*****

One day in 2017, I had coffee with a close girlfriend.

"Why haven't you had kids yet? I know it's something you have wanted ever since I have known you?" she asked.

I was taken aback and felt a mix of regret, embarrassment, and shame. I was unsure how to answer her. The truth was, I had never really tried to make it happen and had just expected it to one day. Something I would hardly admit to myself, let alone voice into the world.

How dumb would I look?
What would she think of me?
Had I been wasting my life away up until that moment?
I should have kids by now! What the heck is wrong with me?

My heart raced and my throat went dry. I felt butterflies in my stomach and couldn't speak. I answered with silence. I felt like a failure, and that weighed heavily on my body. I felt a deep sadness wash over me like I was drowning, and there was no way up. Avoiding her eye contact and waiting for the conversation to change, I remained silent. I knew she wanted me to answer her; there was no getting around it. The silence began to feel suffocating, so I responded, "I don't know." I tried to blink away the tears that were desperately looking for release. What else could I say?

This one conversation, seemingly simple on the surface, triggered a whole series of events, thoughts and realisations I never expected. My self-image was of a woman who was unworthy, not enough, unattractive, overweight, unlovable and useless. I wasn't good enough to have kids, and a complete failure for not having them. My actions and beliefs served as evidence attesting to this. I did nothing to try to fall pregnant, bent over backwards for any guy that showed me even a hint of attention and interest. Already feeling a complete and utter failure in not being able to answer her question honestly, I felt even more of a failure with my whole life.

What the heck have I been doing?

The thought of doing things differently felt incredibly overwhelming. I couldn't even consider other options. My brain felt busy, chaotic, and ready to short-circuit at any moment.

I felt ashamed to show my friend how I was actually feeling and sobbed on the inside. I did as I had always done, which was to sit quietly and offer little to the conversation, hoping a huge hole in the earth would open up and swallow me, or she would change the subject. It didn't, and she didn't. Instead, she asked whether I would consider freezing my eggs. A little taken aback, I hadn't heard of this and felt a burst of excitement race through my body.

This could be the answer to my prayers!

Once again, I avoided the sadness, hurt, anger, and any other negative emotions, leaping at the possibility and hope. That's not to say there's anything wrong with focusing on the positive rather than the negative. In my case, I avoided the negative because it felt so heavy, overwhelming, suffocating and plain hard to deal with if I'm honest. Why wouldn't I want to feel good instead?

After this conversation, it was like my brain switched gears. With little thought beyond "Yep, let me do this and do it now," my full attention went to the steps needed to freeze my eggs.

I was hoping that would fix all the negativity swirling around my mind and body. A simple solution, right? I naively thought at the time that IVF would be a simple and easy process. I was ill-prepared for how big a rollercoaster ride I was about to embark on.

Deciding that IVF was the way forward for me without much else thought, I researched clinics in my local area and read reviews of both the fertility specialists and their success rates.

Statistics provided proof to me that this was the way forward to achieve my desire of becoming a mother. I found a fertility specialist who, by his profile, specialised in IVF for older women and seemed to have good pregnancy success rates.

With little other emotion or thought, I booked an appointment with both my doctor for a referral and the fertility specialist. Looking back, it did feel quite clinical, with a focus on just getting the job done and little regard for the enormity of what I was doing.

A ride that would frustrate, hurt, sadden, depress, overwhelm, inspire, and motivate me, build resilience and self-confidence. It would see me come out of my shell and step into the spotlight, learn to advocate for myself, and pursue my desires regardless of others' opinions about what they believe was best for me.

Interestingly, now that I think about it, no one ever asked me whether I wanted to have children, and I never raised the subject either. I simply hoped and expected that it would happen without any effort on my part. In retrospect, I am not sure how it could have happened when I wasn't actively dating or prioritising finding a partner. I just figured it would all just magically happen (like it does in the movies). Now, movies are an amazing source of enjoyment and inspiration for me, and they are also a form of make-believe. We decide on what we want and then we go after it, don't we? I remember always feeling second best in my relationships and not understanding where this came from (let alone that I even thought this way at that time). Believing that if I said yes to everything, then he'd love/ want/ desire me. Except that never worked, and I repeated the same pattern in relationship after relationship - no wonder I was single for most of my life! Cruising through life with no awareness of self nor the world around me, a bit like living in a fog. No intentional action or thought on my part; instead, I sat back and let life take over. And so life cruised along around me, never fulfilling my desires. Talk about giving my power away!

As soon as I started exploring whether IVF was now the path for me, I felt a shift in my body, a tingling and bubbling of excitement. Blissful unawareness, I call it. I felt so alive, something I hadn't really felt before.

IVF was never something I imagined I would do, and so I knew very little about it. I researched my options about where to go, scouring online for reviews, fertility clinic success rates, and reading others' experiences, all the while still feeling that this was no big deal. I treated it all like a task list.

Do it, and then it's done, no more to worry about. I don't need to know much; the doctors surely know what they were doing and what is best for me. Who am I to question them, let alone interview them to determine their suitability with me and the medication protocols they prescribe me?

I am someone who loves a good checklist, where I read what I need to do, do it, and get the job done. Always in control and holding such a tight grip on things so as not to allow for any spontaneity or veering off my desired path. It also meant I felt emotionally in control.

I would describe myself as a hard worker, methodical, analytical and a people pleaser. I firmly believed that by working hard, often harder than others, I could and would get ahead.

I could do anything I put my mind to and would follow directions to the tee, without question. They (the person giving the directions) were the experts after all. I knew I would make a good mum with so much love to give. Day to day, I worked, went to the gym or took a walk, came home, ate dinner, and then ended the night watching TV. Watching the same TV shows, eating the same few meals all on repeat. Robotic, unintentional, unconscious and unexciting. Can you relate?

Describing my home as a confused canvas, it was a blend of neutrals, splashes of bold and bright colours, all sorts of textures and patterns. In trying to play around with what I liked and build something cohesive (which was my aim), the reality looked more like a hotchpotch of colour and texture. Nothing really went together. My furnishings were opposites and certainly not reflective of a calm, elegant, organised, and purposeful design and were a little like my life at the time, comprising many individual actions and thoughts, without considering the big picture.

I found a reputable doctor/ fertility clinic and booked an appointment with them after obtaining a referral from my doctor.

That was easy!

I felt a nervous excitement about what was to come. I figured that this was my solution. *Freeze my eggs, then later down the track have a baby - simple right?*

Except it wasn't simple at all.

My initial appointment with the fertility specialist Dr Adrian was a meet and greet, before delving straight into my fertility history.

This was our conversation:

Dr Adrian: "How often do you get your period? And how long does your cycle last?"

Me: "Every twenty eight days like clockwork, lasting four to six days"

Dr Adrian: "How would you describe your period?"

Me: "It's a very heavy flow on days one to two, followed by a slight reduction in heaviness by day three and four. Day five is usually a little flow followed by spotting for two days."

Dr Adrian: "What are your premenstrual symptoms?"

Me: "I begin feeling slight cramping four days prior to when I bleed, which sweeps from my right to left side of my stomach. It then remains in the middle of my tummy right up until I start bleeding and then intensifies the first two days of my period. I also get lower back pain, headaches, nausea, tender breasts, crave sweets and carbs and am quite emotional."

Dr Adrian: "Sounds like you may have some endometriosis, have you ever been tested or treated for it?"

Me: "No I haven't"

Dr Adrian: "Have you ever tried to fall pregnant?"

Me: "No I haven't"

Dr Adrian: "Why not?"

Me: (Stunned silence.)

This question floored me. It was a perfectly reasonable question to ask, given I was in an IVF clinic, but damn it stung in my chest when he asked me.

How do I say I just expected it to happen?

I thought my heart was going to burst out of my chest.

"I haven't met the right person," I replied, swallowing the lump in my throat.

An awkward silence followed, though maybe it was just me feeling awkward. He didn't say anything. I was starting to believe it was me and I was the reason I wasn't a mum, again there was something wrong with me. Thankfully the conversation changed to next steps, involving numerous blood tests to check my hormone levels and me taking the pill to further regulate my cycle. This would allow Dr Adrian to predict my cycle and the timing for egg collection with certainty.

 **TIP**

Your intuition is your internal guidance system and will never let you down. If you don't already, spend time regularly tuning into it. I found breathwork the most effective to connect with myself, using slow and deep breaths. You'll notice your heart rate slow, breathing deeper from your stomach, and your mind empty from distracting chatter.

EXERCISE

Breathe in through the nose to a count of 4, hold for a count of 4 and slowly exhale through the mouth to a count of 4. Repeat until you begin to feel a sense of calm in both your body and mind.

Endometriosis and pregnancy

Endometriosis Australia is a nationally accredited charity that raises awareness, educates and funds research for endometriosis.

Endometriosis Australia describes endometriosis as a common disease where tissue similar to the lining of the womb grows outside it in other parts of the body. More than 830,000 (more than 14%) of Australian girls, women, and those assigned female at birth live with endometriosis at some point in their life, with the disease often starting in teenagers. Symptoms are variable and this may contribute to the approximate 6.5 year delay in diagnosis. Common symptoms include pelvic pain that puts life on hold around or during a person's period. It can impact fertility for some but not for all.

There are three kinds of treatments for endometriosis:
1. Medical treatments (medications)
2. Surgical treatments (involving an operation)
3. Complementary treatments (physiotherapy, psychology, complementary medicine, etc.)

Far from being a professional in this space, if you'd like to know more, Endometriosis Australia has a wealth of information on their website or speak with your GP. You can check the back of the book for further details.

After having my blood tests and an internal ultrasound, a follow up appointment with Dr Adrian revealed no major health issues for me to be concerned with. My iron levels were a little low but nothing a slight tweak in my nutrition intake couldn't fix (which it did). The egg collection process would involve me receiving egg-stimulating injections, alongside several early morning blood tests and internal ultrasounds, to measure the quantity and size of the egg follicles.

Easy peasy. Not that I am a fan of needles, but if this is what it takes, then this is what I'll do.

After being handed my script for the injections, I met with the clinic nurse, who was lovely.

Nurse: "Hi Dianne, let's go through the injection protocol and administration together so you feel comfortable before you leave us today."

Me: (Feeling a little nervous and queasy at the thought of needles), "Thank you."

It all seemed so easy. Take the top of the needle off, connect the needle to the syringe, pinch the skin just to the side of my navel and administer the injection. Admittedly feeling squeamish, I did so and once lining the needle up to my skin, I closed my eyes when I pushed the syringe. If I didn't see it, then it wouldn't hurt, right? I was surprised it didn't hurt as much as I had expected; it was more like a blood test prick.

This continued for seven days, with twice-weekly morning blood tests and internal ultrasounds to determine if my egg follicles were growing. Blood tests I was ok with, but the internal ultrasounds felt so invasive, demoralising. Lying on a cold bed with a thin piece of paper covering my body, naked from the waist down, legs in the air. So exposed, vulnerable and awkward. God bless the nurses who tried to make it more comfortable by making small talk and apologising for the coolness of the lubricant on the probe. I caught my breath as the probe was inserted, feeling uncomfortable to say the least. It never got any easier. There is nothing glamorous, delicate or private about this experience. However, it is a necessary part of an IVF cycle, and there's no getting out of it.

My eyes focused on the screen to the side of the nurse to see how many egg follicles I had and what their size was. Anxiety washed over me.

Do I have enough? Are they even a good size? What if I have none or none were good enough, then what?

A wave of relief washed over me as I looked at the numbers on the screen and saw more follicles and that they were growing.

I listened intently to both the doctor and nursing staff at each visit, but didn't really take it all in. I waited with bated breath to hear how many follicles I had and their size, like a wannabe expert, predicting how many I would have for a future embryo transfer. Not for one second did I give any thought to how many would be realistic for my age. I never considered my age to bear any impact on this at all. How naive I was! Dr Adrian told me I had four good-sized egg follicles, measuring over 21 millimetres. This was the benchmark for how many would be collected; anything less than 19 millimetres would not be viable. I was beyond relieved. He was confident they would continue to grow between now and the egg collection date set for one week's time.

Egg collection

In preparation for the egg collection, I started taking the pill so that my menstrual cycle would be even more regular than it usually was, and we would be able to determine with accuracy when I would ovulate. Again, I didn't take much notice of it at the time and would soon come to realise how complex the world of IVF truly is. This was going to well and truly take me out of my comfort zone in more ways than I ever thought possible. It would test my resilience and courage, and I would emerge as a different person at the end (well, return to my true self, not the person I thought I should be or was trying to be for everyone else).

For those unfamiliar with the world of IVF (as I was), the egg retrieval/ collection process is a surgical procedure where eggs (scientifically speaking, oocytes) are removed from the female body, for the purposes of fertilising them and growing them as embryos in the laboratory or snap freezing for future use. Oocyte pick up (OPU), Egg pick up (EPU), egg collection and oocyte collection are all terms commonly used to describe this procedure. Gosh, the acronyms and terms used in IVF can be totally confusing, or is that just me? I've added a glossary at the back to help.

I thought this would be a quick and easy process, leading me to motherhood in no time - if only that were the case! Another blood test to determine where I was in my cycle and when I would ovulate showed my 28-day cycle was on track and I was booked in for day surgery in one week - how exciting! I arranged for a friend to drop me off and pick me up on the day of the procedure. I was all set, or so I thought. So clinical, unemotive and just getting on with the job at hand. Outwardly telling myself, "Di, you have got this". Inwardly, I felt numb to it all, with no thought to what I was doing to myself and my body. I did feel a sense of nerves, as I chose not to disclose at that time to anyone but my friend what I was doing. Fear of judgment, criticism or being talked out of it. I did feel a sense of shame deep down, not consciously so, but it was there. Shame of having to go down the IVF path (fact I didn't have to, I chose to).

So I gave it little thought other than the time I needed to be there, how long my stay would be and any post-recovery support I might need. That was literally it.

For the day procedure itself, I was offered the choice to be awake or asleep. Being none the wiser and quite naive if I am being totally honest, I chose to be asleep. Now I've never had any issues with anaesthetic and I didn't that day. Wheeled into a cold, white, sterile room, Dr Adrian and his team met me. After some quick introductions, he explained that I would fall asleep pretty quickly, which I did, and that I would wake up in the recovery room, which I did. Feeling pretty groggy and quite uncomfortable around my tummy, I was surprised to find myself sitting fairly upright in my chair. A quick bite to eat, I saw Dr Adrian, who told me the egg collection went well and that he collected four eggs, which, for my age (43 years), was pretty good. He also told me that he wasn't sure of their quality, which would be another bridge to cross, but for the moment, all went well, and I felt relieved. Some heat packs and pain relief eased the dull ache I felt around my midsection, and four hours later, I was discharged.

I rested for a while before heading back to my friends' place to sleep for the night. I felt ok, while also quite spaced out. I repeated the conversation with Dr Adrian in my head over and over.

Four eggs were great, but what if the quality wasn't? Was I screwed?

I wasn't really thinking about anything else, apart from how best to manage the pain. Hoping my eggs would be good enough. Again, being quite clinical in my thoughts and actions, I popped a couple of Panadeine Forte and had an early night. I didn't really talk about it with my friend that night. I was trying not to think, as I knew how quickly I could unravel if I did. And I didn't want to feel that, not overwhelmed, anxious, uncomfortable or any kind of emotion. I didn't want to feel anything. So best I didn't think at all and just got on with things. Avoidance at its best.

This was a big deal what I had done, and I didn't really give it much credit at all; it felt more like a task I could tick off my life's checklist. At this time, my family didn't know exactly what I was doing - here's where the shame starts to creep in. They knew I was looking to freeze my eggs, but not the exact date. I headed back to work the next day as though nothing had happened. No one at work knew what I had done, either, actually, very few people did. I was embarrassed to tell anyone, and also didn't want to have to deal with others' judgments, if I'm being honest. Done and dusted, who needed to know anyway? But deep down, I wanted them to know. I wanted them to be part of this journey, my support, cheerleader and champion. I was too afraid to ask.

> ****WHAT IS VITRIFICATION?**
>
> Vitrification is the term used for egg freezing and freezing embryos. Vitrification is similar to snap freezing and removes the risk of ice crystals forming, which can result in cell damage. Eggs or embryos are placed in a special solution (vitrification medium), which is then cooled quickly so that the structure of the water molecule (in the eggs and embryos) doesn't have time to form ice crystals. Instead, it instantaneously solidifies into a glass-like structure.
>
> *Source: Genea Fertility (1986)*

Six months later, I began to pay an egg freezing storage fee. I continued to pay this fee every six months until I was ready to use my eggies. This is a standard process regardless of the fertility clinic you choose. And that was it for the next few years. I continued to cruise through life on autopilot, waiting for my dreams to come true. Not doing much for that to happen, mind you, neither in terms of my thoughts, habits and actions. And so, not much happened: no baby, no partner, and ever-present strong feelings of lack, sadness, and emptiness.

I was turning 46 in June 2020, and I decided this was my year to become a mum. So, I increased my private health cover to top level so pregnancy and related expenses (including IVF) would be covered. Knowing that I would have to wait for twelve months between increasing my cover and starting IVF (and boy, does that twelve months take a long time to come around, or maybe that was just for me), I did this at the start of 2019.

In February 2020, I went to see Dr Adrian with the intention of using my frozen eggs with donor sperm (I was single at this stage). Again, thinking this was a walk in the park, I went into this IVF cycle with my eyes and mind closed, another task on my life checklist to mark off. Funny how behaviours repeat unconsciously. I told my parents about my intention to go ahead with an IVF cycle using my frozen eggs and donor sperm. They were supportive, joined me at my doctor's appointment and asked Dr Adrian about risks associated with me doing the cycle, given my age and what mitigation strategies he would suggest (where possible). I knew Dad was concerned, given his questioning of Dr Adrian, and he wasn't wrong to be. The odds of a successful pregnancy at almost 46 were slim, not impossible, but still, they were less than 5%. They were quite excited, like me, about having a baby, even sharing the news with family and friends. Side note, this was not something I would recommend unless you are happy to share the disappointment as much as you are the success. While it's lovely to have others check in on you and be excited for your journey, it can also be very painful when it doesn't work and you need to tell them (mainly to stop them from asking). I decided that my small inner circle would be the only ones to know about any future cycles.

As I did when freezing my eggs, I underwent a series of blood tests to confirm where I was in terms of my menstrual cycle so that the embryo transfer date could be scheduled. Let's take a step back. For this cycle in using my frozen eggs, Dr Adrian explained I would need to select a sperm donor, and prior to doing so, there were a number of steps to complete. What is an embryo transfer, you ask? It is the final stage of the IVF process where the fertilised egg—now an embryo—is placed in the woman's uterus. The embryo is loaded into a catheter, which is passed through the vagina and cervix and into the uterus, where it is deposited.

Before I go any further, to get there is quite a process, especially if you are using unknown donor sperm, as I was. To begin, I completed genetic testing (this was undertaken via a saliva test, which was posted to me to complete and then return). My fertility clinic used a genetic testing clinic based in the US, so you can imagine it took quite a while for results to come back (six weeks to be exact). This was a mandatory requirement and an additional cost to my IVF cycle, as it involved an external agency completing the testing.

The next step was to undergo three counselling sessions (also mandatory). Again, these were an additional cost to my cycle fees with no rebate from either Medicare or private health insurance. My first counselling session involved discussing my thoughts, feelings and reasoning for undergoing a full IVF cycle.

Counsellor: "Why am I here today, planning to do an IVF cycle?"
Me: "I am single, froze my eggs three years ago and am keen to use them to have a baby"
Counsellor: "How do you feel about doing this on your own, and possibly becoming a single mum?"
Me: "I am fine to do this on my own, and am ok with being a single mum."
Counsellor: "How do you feel about not being successful? Your age puts you in a lower success rate category?"
Me: "I am aware that my age will likely influence success, but I

would rather give it my all than live with the regret of not trying and wondering why if."

Counsellor: "Sounds like you have thought this through and are realistic about what may or may not happen."

Me: "Yes."

Counsellor: "What support do you have to undergo not only this cycle, but if successful, raising a child on your own?"

Me: "I have a small, close-knit group of friends and family who I know will be there for me when and if I need them. They are located geographically close to me, so distance isn't an issue."

Counsellor: "I wish you all the best and can see you have really thought all this through and have people on board you can turn to for emotional support, which is so important."

My second counselling session was to discuss using unknown donor sperm.

Counsellor: "So I am curious why you have decided to use an unknown donor?"

Me: "I haven't had success falling pregnant naturally, am currently single and have been for a while. I am mindful of my age and am looking to become a mum before it can no longer happen."

Counsellor: "Have you tried to find a known donor to use?"

Me: "No, I haven't, my preference would be an unknown donor."

Counsellor: "Ok, how do you feel about your potential child wanting to know about their donor?"

Me: "I have no issue with that and intend from very early on, being transparent with them about their identity and where they can access information should they choose to. I will support them in whatever decision feels right for them."

CHILDHOOD, RELATIONSHIPS & CAREER

Counsellor: "That's very understanding of you. It is important to be open with your potential child early on so it becomes part of general conversations and their story, so as they grow up, it isn't a big deal or a surprise which may later cause conflict."

Me: "I completely agree."

Counsellor: "I wish you all the best."

Both sessions felt and were matter-of-fact. Clearly, I answered the questions correctly, or it was just how the process was meant to be. Don't delve too deep and remain on the surface so they (counsellor) can tick the box to say job done.

My third and final counselling session was in relation to my genetic testing. As with the other two sessions, this was mandatory and provided me with an opportunity to review my results with a genetic nurse. Thankfully, there was no additional fee for this session (phew!)

Genetic nurse: "Hi Dianne, so I have received your genetic test results and am here to discuss them with you. Following our chat, I will send you a list of possible sperm donors for you to select your top three preferences. The donor sperm list I send you will be tailored to match your genetic testing, so there are no clashes that may likely cause any abnormalities or issues. Is that ok?"

Me: "OK, that all sounds good."

Genetic nurse: "OK, so first off, there were no major issues or red flags with your genetic testing results."

"There are a couple of genetic markers which are not a concern unless you use a donor that also has this marker in their genetic profile. That being the case, the list of possible sperm donors that we will send you will not have anyone who has this marker. Apart from

that, there are no other issues to be concerned about or flag."

"Here at our clinic, we use The World Egg Bank for donor sperm, who are based in the United States. The fees are charged in US dollars, and we usually receive the sperm vials within two weeks of purchase."

Me: "That sounds great. I look forward to reviewing the list of possible donors."

Genetic nurse: "Great! Well, I will send you the list in the coming days, please select and email us your top three preferences."

I didn't find the counselling sessions particularly intrusive, but I did want to just get on with it, if I am honest, not that I felt they were a waste of time. It was more my impatience than anything. Now both the genetic testing and payment for sperm donor were in US dollars, and of course I didn't consider the conversion fee at that time, this was how much I wanted to get pregnant and become a mum. Not that this is meant to be an inhibitor for you, but something to consider if you are planning on travelling the IVF path. There are additional costs beyond the cycle fee, and so, some of these may incur international conversion fees. It pays to do your research and budgeting (allowing for a buffer where you can). Prior to beginning IVF, I never considered the financial impact it would have on me. My driving desire for motherhood clouded any other thoughts on the subject, and I was blessed with a healthy bank balance to draw funds from. Depending on where you are in your fertility journey, stage of life, and financial circumstances, you can expect to pay anywhere between $5,000 AUD and $20,000 AUD per cycle. Depending on your individual circumstances, you may be eligible for Medicare and/ or private health fund rebates. I would suggest speaking with your health fund if you are considering the IVF path to give yourself time to meet the waiting periods and also ensure you end up with the most appropriate cover for your needs. The mandatory counselling sessions are approximately $300-$400 per session. These do not attract either a Medicare or private health fund rebate.

 **NOTE**

If you choose to use donor sperm as part of your IVF cycle, there are two options for you - known or unknown donors. The choice is completely yours and a very personal one. From my experience, take your time to make your decision, it is a huge one and not one to be taken lightly. Known donors could include friends, friends of friends, or formal arrangements via a reputable Facebook group.

Using an unknown donor, as was my case, involved accessing a sperm donor bank (yep, that's a real thing). I was able to select certain characteristics that allowed me a degree of personalisation in the selection process. On one hand, it felt strange to be purchasing some random guy's sperm; on the other, it would get me one step closer to motherhood. Like many clinics, I was able to buy enough sperm for each cycle only. This reduced the need to outlay the cost of a number of straws (the name given to the sperm being purchased) at the beginning of treatment, which were unlikely to be required. So many terms, procedures and timelines to wrap my head around. I soon became an expert at all things IVF, a downside to undergoing numerous cycles.

As promised, the genetic nurse emailed me six donor profiles for me to select from. It felt a bit like reading someone's dating profile, except there was so much more information available (which is incredibly helpful!). I had access to:

- Full medical history of the donor, his parents and grandparents (on both sides),
- Hobbies
- Interests
- Education
- Aspirations
- Whether he'd had any prior pregnancies (i.e. had he gotten anyone pregnant before making his donation)
- Why did he chose to donate
- A message to his potential future offspring

As my donor choices were located in the US, I was blessed to see both baby and adult photos of them. Having access to these greatly helped me in making my choice of who would be the best donor for me. Be mindful that not all donor clinics will provide you with baby and adult photos of the donors. It very much depends on where you are sourcing your donor from. It is a lot to take in, I know, and it pays to take your time and be gentle with yourself throughout the journey.

When choosing my donor, my preference was someone with a good health history (on both sides of his family) first and foremost, followed by a similar cultural background to me. Sure, their height was a consideration (I'm 162cm, so I would like someone taller) but it wasn't a priority. I wanted a healthy donor whom I felt would, in turn, help pass on healthy genes to my baby. My baby's gender was also not really an issue for me in terms of gender preference, as long as they were healthy, that was what mattered most to me. I took the time to study and think deeply about each donor, considering their suitability and, more importantly, why. Why am I choosing them above the others? How does the choice feel in my body?

I selected a male aged in his late 20's, no major health issues in his family, sporty, wide ranging hobbies and interests. He'd had two prior reported pregnancies and had a lovely, friendly smile. He felt like the right choice for me. Now I should add here that when I say he had two reported pregnancies; there wasn't further information in his profile regarding live births. On one hand that would be good to know as it shows sperm health and quality, on the other hand it is also confidential.

So sperm donor selected (tick), mandatory counselling sessions completed (tick), genetic testing completed and results received (tick), I was well on my way to becoming a mum (or so I thought). I paid for my donor sperm, and luckily, it was available to use straight away. A sign of luck, perhaps?

**NOTE

Most fertility clinics keep reserves of US-based donor sperm at their clinics in Australia. Clinics often purchase numerous vials of sperm to be shipped here and used in IVF cycles, as was in my case. This does bring the cost down slightly, and most importantly the wait time.

The nurses at my fertility clinic were lovely and kept me informed with each step of the process about what I needed to do. I figured if I did as I was told, it would all turn out. I should mention costs at this point, as it is widely known how expensive IVF is (especially when doing multiple cycles). Private Health insurance (top level) will often cover a lot of expenses such as the egg collection and embryo transfer procedures. Medicare may reduce the cost of the medications used, but there is still an out-of-pocket payment to be made and that is still in the thousands (eek!). Dr Adrian handed me a quote for the cycle, which included thawing my eggs, fertilising them using the donor sperm I had purchased (separately) and then the embryo transfer. Medications would be an additional fee charged by the pharmacy. The total cost would be $20,800! While I would be eligible to claim a portion of costs from my private health insurer, I would receive no rebate from Medicare. This was because it was my choice to do IVF, and not a related health or fertility issue. Reading the quote, I would essentially be paying for everything out of pocket.

I bought and began to take the medications prescribed to me at the times I was advised to. I also took a variety of supplements with the intention of increasing both my egg quality and the number of eggs I produced. The date was set to defrost my frozen eggs from 2017, fertilise them with the donor sperm and then wait for the embryo to develop, ready for implantation. This process was expected to take approximately 5 days, from the start (thawing my eggs) to implantation. Dr Adian told me there were risks with my eggs not surviving the thawing process, they also may not fertilise, and the embryo may not divide into enough cells to proceed with implantation. Who knew this was so complex? I kept my fingers crossed that everything would go to plan. There were several checkpoints I desperately wanted to reach.

There was a raft of risks, including gestational diabetes, preeclampsia, Down syndrome or other genetic disorders, miscarriage or premature birth or low birth weight. It was a lot to digest, while also not panicking at something that hadn't even happened yet. These risks are fairly common ones, albeit a little higher for me due to my age. While IVF has come a long way, there is no guarantee, and science can only do so much. Genetics also plays a significant role.

Step one was defrosting the four frozen eggs I had from 2017. If none of them survived the thawing process, that would be the end of my cycle. I desperately hoped that some, if not all, had survived the thawing. I was beyond relieved the next day when the nurse told me that three of the four had survived.

Step two was to fertilise the eggs with the donor sperm and see if they were fertilised by the next morning. An embryologist performed the fertilisation process and was to advise of the outcome. I nervously waited to hear; it felt a lot longer than just 24 hours. When the embryologist rang to tell me that two eggs had been successfully fertilised, resulting in two embryos, I was overjoyed.

Step three was to wait and see if the embryos continued to develop and divide, progressing to implantation. It was all a waiting game, full of emotional highs and lows, anxiously waiting, praying for a favourable outcome, and not watching the clock, or I'd go crazy. By this stage, I was scheduled for the embryo transfer on the following Monday morning. To confirm this, she said she would call me on the Saturday and provide an update.

*****

Saturday morning came and filled with optimism I headed out shopping with my parents. While I was out, the embryologist called, and I was excited to hear from her.

Embryologist: "Hi Dianne, I'm calling to talk with you about your upcoming embryo transfer on Monday"

Me: "OK great, what time would you like me in".

Embryologist: "Umm, the embryos have not progressed as much as I would like. That's not to say they won't by Monday, but the chances are fairly slim. I just wanted to let you know so if we cancel Monday it's not a total surprise for you. I will check back in with you early Monday morning and we'll go from there".

My heart sank. I found it hard to swallow the emotional lump in my throat. Tears welled in my eyes in the middle of the shopping centre. I didn't want to be here. I just wanted to head home, hide away in my room and cry. This was not what was meant to happen.

"Thank you for the update, I appreciate it and hope there's progress over the weekend," I managed.

Mum and Dad who had been out of earshot started walking towards me and I burst into tears. I struggled to speak but managed through tears to tell my parents what had happened. They were understandably apologetic and supportive. I felt devastated, deeply devastated.

We drove home in a sad silence. My heart was breaking that I couldn't even have the chance to fall pregnant. I felt like it was all over before it could even begin.

The remainder of the weekend was fairly uneventful. I felt sad, numb, and was praying for a miracle to come on Monday morning. Monday morning came around and I anxiously awaited the phone call. I had already booked the day off work expecting to be having an embryo transfer. I was now not sure if that would be the case, but desperately hoped it would be. 9am came around and the phone rang.

Embryologist: "Hi Dianne, I wanted to give you an update. As we discussed on Saturday the embryos have not grown as much as I would like, and they are not viable for transfer. I'm so sorry, please know that we have a counselling service available to you whenever you are ready to help you process all that has happened."

In my heart I wasn't surprised. Deep down I had known on Saturday this cycle was now over and I would need to start all over again. Numb, sad and hugely disappointed in myself I thanked her for calling and retreated to my room for the rest of the day. I just needed to be by myself. I should have had my baby transferred to me, and instead, I had nothing.

Now I'm not sure about you, but maybe you have also gone through an IVF people and like me, told people. I now found myself in the position of needing to tell them I had failed (so I thought anyway). Feelings of shame, embarrassment, and a fear of others' judgment, along with a reluctance to discuss it, all crept in. I left it until later that day to tell them my cycle was now over. I kept it pretty matter-of-fact, all the while trying to keep my emotions together and not burst into tears (not an easy thing to do). I no longer wanted to share with so many people; the aftermath of having it all fall over just felt like too much to have to explain.

"Failure is inevitable, but how you deal with it matters,"

— TODD HENRY

 **NOTE**

According to the Victorian Assisted Reproductive Authority (VARTA), the younger you are when you start IVF, the more likely you are to have a baby.

Woman's age at first IVF cycle	Chance of baby after first cycle	Chance of baby after second cycle	Chance of baby after third cycle
Under 30	43%	59%	66%
30-31	48%	61%	67%
32-33	44%	60%	67%
34-35	40%	54%	61%
36-37	32%	44%	50%
38-39	22%	32%	38%
40-41	13%	21%	25%
42-43	6%	10%	11%
44+	2%	5%	5%

Source: Victorian Assisted Reproductive Authority (n.d.) Most women overestimate their chance of IVF success.
https://libraryguides.vu.edu.au/apa-referencing/7Webpages

As you can see, success rates are significantly less once a woman reaches her 40's but it was not entirely impossible. I bring this up, as I look back and wish I had started so much younger, even if just to freeze my eggs. It seems our 20s is the ideal age to do so, when our eggs are in good health and in abundant supply. For me, I spent my 20s travelling the world and working overseas, I never even contemplated making such a decision. I wish I had! A disclaimer that whether you decide to start in your 20's, 30's or 40's there is still no guarantee it'll work. And there is nothing wrong with you whatever you decide. This is purely me reflecting on what I may have done differently in the past.

I was at a total loss. My first IVF cycle was a dismal failure (note the negative self talk creeping in). In reality I didn't do anything wrong, I gave it my best shot. Funny how we turn inwards to berate and chastise ourselves so easily when we wouldn't dare to do the same with our child or a loved one. And this in a nutshell is the emotional roller coaster that is IVF.

"Expect great things and great things will come"

– NORMAN VINCENT PEAL

"Now what do I do?" I wondered. I went back to Dr Adrian, maybe he had the answers. He said I could begin a new cycle and collect fresh eggs to use for a fresh embryo transfer. The cycle where I defrosted my eggs, paid for donor sperm ($2,000 AUD), used the sperm to fertilise my eggs, and medications which cost me a total of $1800. Had the embryo grown and we had gone ahead with the scheduled embryo transfer the total cycle cost would have been $19800. The biggest portion being the embryo transfer. Why the price difference?

As the embryos never really grew, I didn't have to pay for the embryologist, nor the transfer procedure. Both of which were the highest costs in the cycle overall. Dr Adrian's fees were quite high, which at the time I thought was just how much IVF cost. I soon learnt that was not the case and I was misclassified under Medicare which affected how much I could claim back.

I went back to Dr Adrian's office to discuss the chance of a second attempted transfer. My excitement and nervousness were building.

Maybe this time round it will work. Maybe it's all just about timing?

Dr Adrian outlined the process for me. It would be starting from the beginning all over again:

1. Contact the clinic nurse on day one of my menstrual cycle and confirm I want to use the same donor sperm.
2. Collect prescribed injections (Gonal-f, Orgalutran and Ovidrel) and commence taking Gonal-f.
3. Track my menstrual cycle via two to three blood tests and two internal ultrasounds to determine my date of ovulation, number and size of egg follicles suitable for collection.
4. Pay for donor sperm.
5. Schedule egg collection date (three days prior to the actual egg collection procedure). Continue taking Gonal-f in addition to Orgalutran. Doing so would cause ovulation and aid in egg collection preparation.

6. Prepare for egg collection, taking the Ovidrel trigger injection to aid the final maturation of my eggs prior to ovulation and egg collection. Ovidrel would be taken three days prior to egg collection.
7. Attend egg collection procedure (day ten of my menstrual cycle).
8. Dr Adrian would advise the number of eggs collected.
9. Embryologist to fertilise collected eggs (same day as egg collection procedure).
10. Embryologist to advise the number of embryos created following fertilisation (the day following the egg collection procedure).
11. Schedule embryo transfer procedure (roughly three to five days following egg collection procedure). The exact timing depends on the number of cells the embryo develops and the age of the patient. In my case, given I was mid-40s my embryo transfers were all day three.
12. Attend embryo transfer.
13. Final blood test confirming pregnancy (two weeks following embryo transfer).

Wow! I didn't realise how involved a full cycle would be, mainly because I had only done the first half previously when freezing my eggs. It was a calculated science that is intensive, thorough, and involves numerous moving parts. Following my visit, Dr Adrian emailed me a copy of his quote for approximately $20,000 to do a full cycle. Medications would be an additional cost of roughly $200.

As I considered both the timing and costs of this next cycle,

COVID-19 reared its head in Australia. Initial media reports were full of panic, uncertainty and scaremongering. Uncertainty in terms of what this meant for my everyday life. In the beginning I wasn't too worried as I thought it would all just settle down and life would continue as it had always done. It was only a matter of weeks later I received an email from my fertility clinic stating that all new IVF procedures in New South Wales were cancelled until further notice. Shock, sadness and disbelief hit that I was just about to commence a cycle and now nothing. Had I had been in the middle of or had commenced a cycle, I would have been allowed to proceed. In my case, because I hadn't yet started, it was over before it could begin.

Shit! Worry soon knocked on my door, followed by tears of frustration. I had no idea when I would be able to commence a cycle. *What if it was too late?* Regret and anger soon followed. I questioned myself. *Why had I left it until my forties to even begin trying for a baby? Why was life so cruel to give on one hand and then take with the other?*

I cannot emphasise the impact of negative self talk and how heavy it feels in your body, especially your heart. It alone can create more damage to self than what anyone else can say to you. This is one of the reasons why self-image and personal development are so important to me. I know first-hand the damage a negative self-image can cause and how life-changing switching up our thoughts can be. My thoughts in those moments were causing me to spiral:

"*Why am I being punished?*"
"*Am I not meant to be a mum?*"

"Why do bad things always happen to me?"
"What is wrong with me?"

In truth, there was no one to blame. I had done nothing wrong, and as I was soon to learn, when the universe takes with one hand it gives with another.

Like many others here in Australia and around the globe, I had no idea about this virus called COVID-19 and just how big an impact it would have on all our lives for the next two and a half years. So, that was it; there was nothing more to do now, other than wait, and wait I did. Full of hope, desire, and impatience that it wouldn't take long for life and IVF to resume back to normal. Desperately hoping it wouldn't be too long before I could begin another cycle and have my longed-for baby. Life went on (albeit in a new world of lockdowns) and I waited…

During this time I began to see a fertility nutritionist and a naturopath to help me prepare my body as best I could for a future cycle. This included having blood tests to check my hormone level baseline. These uncovered that I was prone to inflammation, which explained the bloating I experienced. I learnt that inflammation could pose resistance to any IVF cycle being successful. This led me to choose to eliminate gluten and dairy (known inflammatory triggers). I also began taking supplements to help reduce existing internal inflammation and increase my iron and folate levels. Again, I did so without question, they advised me what I should be taking, I bought it and began taking it - no questions asked. I didn't consider whether my body actually needed any of these supplements, I blindly believed they were the experts. Who was I to question them?

Within the first four weeks of removing gluten and dairy from my diet I noticed a dramatic increase in my energy levels, skin texture and glow, hair strength and shine. I had a significant reduction in bloating and heaviness in my tummy and I lost four kilos without even trying just ceasing intake of gluten and dairy based foods.

Four months passed and I was beyond elated to read in the news that IVF was allowed to resume. I contacted my fertility clinic to arrange another consultation with Dr Adrian to review the earlier quote and schedule to begin a full cycle. The phone lines were busy so I had to leave a message. Not surprising given I was probably not the only one looking to commence a cycle. More waiting!

My fertility clinic called the next day to advise that Dr Adrian had moved to another fertility company. If I wanted to move with him I was more than welcome to, alternatively, I could move to another doctor within the same clinic and complete my next cycle for a reduced price. I was shocked to say the least, like seriously, couldn't life just be easy this once? This turn of events turned out to be a blessing in disguise.

Wanting to consider all of my options, I requested a list of alternate doctors' names and their profiles. I received an email from my clinic a few hours later with the information I had requested. I googled their profiles straight away, searching for client reviews and success rates. This was what mattered most to me, in addition to whether they specialised in older women, which although I hated to admit it, I was.

This was something I had not expected in the least. I was

more than a little peeved that Dr Adrian had not bothered to contact any of his existing patients to let them know what had happened, wondering if there was more to the story. Funnily enough, as I was thinking about this, he called me. His swift departure from the clinic sounded dubious, but it is what it is. He gave me his recommendation of two doctors within the fertility clinic he felt would be suitable for me should I choose to stay. While I did find it helpful to have my choice narrowed down based on his professional opinion, I was also more than a little wary, given how he had handled his move to another company. Trusting my gut at this time, I did my research and found that one of the doctors he had recommended, specialised in IVF for women over 40 (yay!), and I read online about many positive experiences from other women he had worked with, women who were in my age range. And he was located fairly close to me should I choose to go with him.

This was a big decision for me as I am not the sort of person who jumps from doctor to doctor on a whim. On one hand I knew and had worked with Dr Adrian, felt comfortable with him and his competence as an IVF specialist. There was also a part of me considering whether someone new would have more luck with me (new shiny toy syndrome) and I felt torn. To ease my restless mind, I made an appointment to see Dr Lee to see what vibe I got from him, what he suggested in terms of medication protocols for me and what the cost would be. Dr Adrian had already outlined the costs of around $20,000 to resume a cycle with him, with no Medicare rebate and a partial rebate from my private health insurer. This was a big decision and one I didn't take lightly.

Speaking with Dr Lee I discovered I was actually entitled to a Medicare rebate due to my age (I was considered 'socially infertile' - what a terrible term!), which equated to significant savings across a full IVF cycle.

Dr Lee: "Should you choose to do your IVF cycle with me, you would probably be looking at an out-of-pocket expense of about $5,000 to $6,000 considering both your Medicare and private health fund rebates."

Me: "Wow!"

I liked the energy of Dr Lee and his straightforwardness, wondering if he might be the one to help me realise my desire for motherhood. I won't lie, the cost difference was significant and something to consider rather than just disregard.

My decision of which doctor to go with came down to the following reasons:

★ Success rate using fresh eggs by women aged over 40

★ Medication protocol, considering I had entered perimenopause

★ Positive experiences by friends of friends who spoke highly of Dr Lee

★ His willingness to listen to my wants, needs and questions

★ Reduced cost (I won't lie, this did factor in my final decision, although it was lower on the priority list)

I gave myself a week to digest the information from Dr Adrian and Dr Lee, wanting to avoid rushing in for the sake of it, while also knowing there was a big part of me just wanting to get on with the job. During that week, I found myself leaning closer towards Dr Lee, yet found the idea of letting Dr Adrian go a little unnerving.

"What if I make the wrong decision?"
"What if I fail?"
"What is the right decision?"
"Why can't someone just tell me what to do?"

To find the answer to my questions I sought the advice of tarot cards, hoping they would tell me what to do. This added even more confusion as I got a different answer each time. I was looking outside of me for the answers to my life.

After going back and forth for what felt like longer than a week, I decided to go with Dr Lee. Similar to what Dr Adrian had already told me, there would be a number of steps before I would be at the pregnancy test stage.

Dr Lee: "I will be prescribing Gonal-f, Orgalutran and Ovidrel for this cycle and we will see how you go with it before we look at making any changes. These are the best medications for a woman of your age. Your eggs are not the best as you are now over 40 when women's fertility declines. But we can try and see what we can do for you."

Me: "Oh ok, I am keen to begin, how soon can we make that happen?"

Dr Lee: "I understand. Have you thought at all about donor eggs. There are groups where you can advertise to find a known donor. You may have more luck with a younger woman's eggs. It's still not guaranteed, but the chances are shown to improve dramatically. In the meantime, I will draft up a quote for you to go over and if you decide to accept, I will ask you to please contact the clinic nurse on day one of your menstrual cycle and we will go from there. The quote I will send you will reflect the reduced fee for choosing to stay with our clinic."

Me: "Ok that all sounds good, I look forward to receiving your quote, inclusive of the reduced fee for me choosing to stay with the same clinic."

I received the quote, inclusive of the reduced fee later the same day, quite efficient! It read as the doctor had verbally outlined to me, and I chose to sleep on it before signing and returning it to the clinic the next day.

The steps I would follow this cycle were:

1. Contact the clinic nurse day one of my menstrual cycle and confirm I wanted to use the same donor sperm I had used with Dr Adrian.
2. Collect prescribed injections (Gonal-f, Orgalutran and Ovidrel) and commence taking Gonal-f.
3. Track my menstrual cycle via two to three blood tests and two internal ultrasounds to determine my date of ovulation, number and size of egg follicles suitable for collection.
4. Pay for donor sperm.
5. Schedule egg collection date (three days prior to the actual egg collection procedure). I would continue taking Gonal-f in addition to Orgalutran. This would cause me to ovulate and prepare my body for the egg collection.
6. Prepare for egg collection, adding Ovidrel trigger injection to trigger final maturation of my eggs prior to ovulation and egg collection. Ovidrel would be taken three days prior to egg collection.
7. Attend egg collection procedure (day ten of my menstrual cycle).
8. Dr Lee would advise the number of eggs collected

9. The embryologist would fertilise collected eggs (same day as egg collection procedure).
10. The embryologist would advise the number of embryos created following fertilisation (the day following the egg collection procedure).
11. Schedule embryo transfer procedure (roughly three to five days following egg collection procedure).
12. Attend embryo transfer.
13. Final blood test confirming pregnancy (two weeks following embryo transfer).

You may be asking at this point why I was undergoing an IVF cycle as opposed to the many other options within the world of IVF. The simple reason is that I wasn't a suitable candidate for Intrauterine Insemination (IUI). IUI is a procedure that involves placing the sperm into the uterus using a small tube prior to ovulation. This is a somewhat 'gentler' approach but usually requires excellent quality eggs and sperm to be successful. That should have given me a big hint that my eggs were not 'quality'. Given I was in my mid-40s by this stage, IVF was my best chance for success as my eggs were deemed a lower quality purely based on my age. So, with limited time, Dr Lee advised that IVF was the most viable option for me. This was new to me as Dr Adrian had never mentioned anything other than an IVF cycle to me and why this would be the best option for me. I also didn't look into it in much depth, which was my error and responsibility.

An IVF cycle using a woman's own eggs is defined where fertility medication (such as Gonal-f, Ovidrel and Orglautran) stimulates the ovaries to produce a larger number of eggs that are then removed from the ovaries and combined with the donated sperm in the laboratory to fertilise. After fertilisation, the embryo develops in the laboratory for three to five days and is then transferred back to the woman's uterus. With a better understanding of what I was choosing and why, I felt good proceeding with Dr Lee to do a full IVF cycle and become a mum.

All up I underwent four cycles with Dr Lee using my own eggs. The first, second and fourth cycles all resulted in chemical pregnancies. A chemical pregnancy (sometimes called biochemical pregnancy) is a very early pregnancy loss which usually happens just after the embryo implants (before or around 5 weeks). The third resulted in a very painful miscarriage. Across the first three cycles, my medication protocol remained the same and each transfer I felt the same symptoms during the two week wait (this is where you wait, albeit patiently, to have your pregnancy test). Nausea, sore boobs, tiredness, bloating, and sharp cramps the first 3-5 days following transfer. Yes these are possible pregnancy symptoms but they are also possible medication side effects. I truly believe (and still do) that my precious embryos were implanted and were unable to stick for want of a better term.

Each time I felt I had failed and desperately asked for answers on what I could do differently. Each time, Dr Lee told me that the problem was with my old eggs and that it would be best to just move on to using donor eggs - boy if it was only that simple! Letting go of the idea of not having a biological child was not as easy as he was making it out to be. That was quite a heavy emotional process to swim through. There was no consideration to change medications, as he felt it wouldn't make a difference.

My question was, 'Couldn't we at least try?'.

The fourth cycle we did try a different medication protocol, termed a long down cycle. This included using a drug called Synarel, a nasal spray used to help decrease the amount of FSH and LH hormones that your body produces. The purpose of me taking Synarel was to help control the release of eggs from my ovaries and is also used to treat endometriosis (in case there were any remnants left following my earlier surgery).

In females, follicle stimulating hormone (FSH) and another hormone called luteinising hormone (LH) help control the menstrual cycle (periods). FSH helps with ovulation — when an egg is released each month by the ovaries. The amount of FSH varies throughout the menstrual cycle. It is at the highest level just before ovulation.

I began taking Synarel for approximately five weeks before I began my other injections (again Gonal-f, Orgalutran and Ovidrel). It was the worst five weeks of my life. The nausea I felt from taking Synarel was beyond extreme. Synarel would assist in decreasing the amount of oestrogen produced by my ovaries, which would provide a more controlled situation for subsequent stimulation of the ovaries to produce eggs.

This became my first taste of advocating for myself. I wish I had stood up for myself sooner, something I have since promised myself I would never stop doing, and haven't to date. If you haven't gone through the IVF process I'll share a quick rundown of what happens, timings and rough cost. For expert opinion, please consult your own fertility specialist as what I am sharing is purely my experience.

The first procedure (checkpoint was my name for it) is the egg retrieval. In preparation, this involved two to three blood tests beginning the day I started bleeding (day one of my menstrual cycle), as well as again approximately midway through my cycle (roughly day ten) to check when I was due to ovulate. Then there were two internal ultrasounds to ascertain the number and size of my egg follicles, tracking their growth over approximately seven to ten days. This is key information for the egg retrieval procedure. It helps determine when it'll happen, if it'll happen and the likelihood for an embryo transfer. Quality really does matter here; the higher the quality of the egg follicles, the greater the chance of quality eggs, which would provide a greater likelihood of me progressing to embryo transfer. It really is all a numbers game at the end of the day. One I was willing to bet on every time.

What I will acknowledge now is how easy it can be for the world of IVF and trying for a baby to consume you each and every cycle. My first cycle with Dr Lee, I went in with a plan to follow the directions I was given. There were no questions asked, and I was sure I would have a baby. In my head it was literally that simple. Except it didn't happen that way, nor did the second and third cycles either. Changing doctors from Dr Adrian to Dr Lee wasn't a magic fix. Acupuncture wasn't a magic fix. Supplements to improve the quality of my eggs weren't a magic fix. Choosing to eliminate dairy and gluten from my diet wasn't a magic fix. Introducing meditation into my nightly sleep routine wasn't a magic fix.

All I wanted to know was that I needed to do to make it happen. I would have done anything to have my beloved baby.

The spiralling thoughts were neverending in my brain:

"How many follicles are there?"

"Is the size ok?"

"Will I even make it to embryo transfer?"

Repetitive, anxious and fearful ruminations swirled around my head, when in reality there wasn't much I could do to control any of it. Sure I could assist my chances of success and support my body overall by eating well, reducing my stress levels and taking a variety of supplements, all with the intent to increase both the number and size of the egg follicles. Even then, it was still all out of my control, which I didn't like one bit.

I constantly questioned myself.

Does it really make a difference given my age at the time I started IVF? The idea of not following the strict diet and supplementing was not an option; I didn't want to take the risk and have something that I did or didn't do cost me the chance of becoming a mum.

In some ways I think it did help. My body felt lighter physically and I could clearly see a huge difference in my skin and hair texture - that must have meant I was doing something right, didn't it? In other ways I believe it added to my stress levels and took me down a path where I felt my actions were the magic answer. In short, there is no magic answer. Life pretty much revolved around every cycle. What I ate (or didn't), how I spent my time, who I spent it with (or didn't). My life fully revolved around IVF and everything else fell by the wayside. My social interactions significantly reduced. I was laser focused on my nutrition, supplements, exercise and natural therapies such as meditation, acupuncture, chinese herbs, and supplements. My time, energy, focus, finances all went towards this. Nothing else mattered to me at that time.

For three of my four IVF cycles with Dr Lee, we collected four good-sized eggs each round, which, when fertilised, created two embryos. I had both embryos implanted for each of these three cycles. In my fourth cycle only one egg was collected; a poor quality egg at that. Dr Lee gave me a fifty per cent chance of it even fertilising with the donor sperm. I felt heartbroken.

What went so wrong this time round? Sure, the Synarel made me nauseous all day every day but it was supposed to help me, not give me less than I had before.

I desperately wanted a baby, so I took the risk and felt good about it. In spite of the low odds, I still had a fifty per cent chance of success, so I bet on myself. The cycle continued and I was elated to hear my egg had successfully fertilised. I now had everything crossed and an embryo would be implanted and stuck. Feeling the odds were in my favour, I cheered when the embryologist called to tell me that my precious embryo was growing. More than a few tears were shed when the nurse rang to schedule me in for embryo transfer three days later. I felt incredibly proud of myself for taking such a big risk and trusting in my capabilities. Surely this meant success, right?

I took the day off work to have the embryo implanted plus the following day to be able to give my body a rest after all she had done for me. It was the least I could do. And rest I did, lying on the lounge; reading, napping - just slowing down and savouring what I was hoping to come (a positive pregnancy test).

I was due to have a blood test in twelve days to determine if I was pregnant. I obsessed over every symptom or change in my body, convinced it meant I was pregnant. I felt nauseous, had tender breasts, headaches, strong cramping the first three days and strong fatigue. Sure, it could well have been the IVF medications I, but I truly felt like I was pregnant - sixth sense maybe? For three days post embryo transfer I continued injecting Ovidrel to aid implantation. What I soon noticed though, not long after I stopped taking the Ovidrel, roughly day five post transfer, my symptoms disappeared literally overnight.

What the heck was happening? I tried to convince myself all was okay, but deep down I was worried about what this could mean. I hoped it meant nothing.

Maybe I am just overreacting?

The two week wait in between embryo transfer and the pregnancy blood tests is the longest gap of time ever. Waiting to hear I am pregnant. Waiting to see that my body responds with open arms to this precious embryo. Waiting to find out I don't bleed this month because I'm pregnant. Waiting, waiting, waiting. The day finally arrived for me to have my blood test. I decided to go in early and do it before work, hoping that meant I would get my results back early. Optimistically I headed to the collection centre, not bleeding so maybe today was the day. Arriving ten minutes before they opened, I found a parking spot right outside the collection centre and stood at the door first in line. I cheered inside.

Looking at my watch I noticed it was 7.55am, only five more minutes to go. At that moment I felt a strange sensation through my lower body, was I bleeding? As a woman who has menstruated for many decades, I know the sensation of when my bleeding is about to start and that's exactly what it felt like. My heart sank, surely, I haven't gotten this close for it to be taken away. I could now feel the bleeding and I knew in my heart I wasn't pregnant, standing at the door with a few minutes to go till opening, no one else around me.

Do I even bother staying to do the blood test, clearly I am not pregnant?

I knew the answer, the clinic would tell me yes to do the blood test anyway and so I waited. I rang a bestie in tears. By now I knew I was bleeding and cramping had also shown itself. Numb, sad and disappointed, I had the blood tests and headed to work. I knew I wouldn't get the results until early afternoon so I tried to keep myself busy and distracted at work, grateful there was a lot to do to keep my attention and focus.

The hours passed quite quickly and then my phone rang. It was my fertility clinic and I was sure by now that my test would come back negative for a pregnancy.

The nurse who called me was lovely.

Nurse: "Hi Dianne, I'm just calling with your blood test results."
Me: "Hi, how are you?"
Nurse: "I'm good thanks, I am guessing you may already know your result. Am so sorry, you are not pregnant this cycle."
Me: "Thanks for letting me know."

I felt numb, sad and shit.

Nurse: "As you know we do have counsellors available I can connect you with if you would like?"
Me: "Yes, thank you I am aware of that. I will reach out in a few days to talk with someone. Thank you for your call."
Nurse: "No problem at all, if you would like to discuss your result with Dr Lee, please call his admin to make an appointment."
Me: "I will, thank you."

And that was it. I wasn't pregnant, felt like crap and didn't want to be at work, anywhere really other than at home. Why is this so hard? I felt totally defeated at that stage. What else could I be doing? Notice here how it sounds so action-oriented? Where was I caring for myself, my thoughts and loving habits? That appeared to be non-existent. I felt like punching a wall and falling down in a heap to bawl my eyes out, possibly both at the same time. My mind was all over the place and I just didn't know what to feel or what to do. Why was life being so cruel?

Self-image is a powerful force that can both elevate and sabotage, depending on how we think, believe, act and live. Mine at best wasn't that positive to start with, so you can probably imagine the toll IVF was taking on me physically, emotionally and mentally. I was questioning my worth, my decisions to date, which culminated in a very anxious, stressed, frustrated and lost woman. I felt like a complete and utter failure and was too ashamed to even divulge this to those closest to me. What would they think? Perhaps they felt the same way about me and didn't want to say anything. I didn't show up for me. I did what I had always done; I put myself last, telling myself I could get to my needs another day. There were more important things to focus on. I stopped taking care of myself, no longer focusing on eating well and moving every day. Good nutrition was replaced by takeaway, processed foods or not eating at all. There was no intentionality to my life.

Why bother anyway? It's not like it would make any difference if I did.

I stayed up until all hours of the night, knowing full well it would leave me exhausted, irritable and sluggish the next day.

I cancelled social plans to stay locked indoors. I stopped choosing me.

My thoughts were beginning to spiral. I know that those closest to me have always wanted the best for me and have consistently supported me. The judgemental thoughts swirling around my head were mine and mine alone. No one was labelling me as a failure, useless, worthless; I was doing that all on my own.

What the heck was IVF doing to me?

I had become so consumed by it all, I literally ate, drank and slept based on what would give me the greatest chance of success. Was I alone in this behaviour? Working full time, attending weekly acupuncture appointments, twice weekly blood tests, weekly ultrasounds, and talking with the nurses once to twice weekly. The remaining time left I cooked, cleaned, visited family and slept. What a life!

I have lost count of the number of women I have spoken to who have felt the same; consumed by the world of IVF. For some, it has ruined relationships, devastated families financially, let alone the mental anguish when, at the end of it all, it isn't successful. Then what? I wondered how I would balance the desire for motherhood, travel down the IVF path and come out sane at the other end, regardless of the outcome. I believe this is an individual journey and a very personal one at that. For me it evolved over time (and cycle, and fertility specialist).

For all four cycles, I was taking a multitude of supplements, having weekly if not twice weekly acupuncture sessions and had made the choice to become gluten and dairy free in order to reduce any likelihood of internal inflammation. Inflammation is a known influence in unsuccessful embryo transfers. This was on advice from my naturopath and I have to admit that within four weeks of doing so, I felt a new woman. Gone were the dull skin and hair, brittle nails, feeling sluggish. Replaced with an increase in energy levels and clear, bright and healthy looking skin (YAY). I was also regularly drinking bone broth and green smoothies (quite delicious despite the colour) on advice from my acupuncturist. If this wasn't helping to detox, heal and rejuvenate my body then I didn't know what would. It's as if I felt that by doing all of this, then it would miraculously help me become a mum. Gosh, if only it were the case.

Looking back now I can clearly see just how much I was doing externally to help me have my longed-for baby. What I wasn't doing (or hadn't even thought of) was the internal work. I should disclose here that this has always been the case for me, i.e. fix the external and not focus on the internal feelings and so on. Case in point: at one time in my life I lost twenty-three kilograms in weight. I was going to the gym four times a week doing circuit training, weight and cardio classes all the while following the CSIRO diet. It worked for me, and I lost weight in about six months. What I never considered was how I may then see myself differently, going from a size fourteen to a size eight. I can tell you hand on heart that when I looked in the mirror following such big weight loss I didn't see any difference, even though I fitted into smaller size clothing. I still saw the worthless, not good enough women who used to be a size fourteen. The physical body had changed, the mental and emotional had not. The same applied to my IVF path. And it wasn't until I started to reflect back on the early years of my life, that I started to understand.

Early Childhood

I grew up in the early 1970s in a suburban home to two loving parents, a younger sister, and fur sibling Tammy. I mentioned Tammy as she was extremely important to my childhood and had a lasting influence on me still to this day. Memories of my childhood included playing in the yard with Tammy (Tamby as I called her) chasing balls, constructing forts from old cardboard boxes dad brought home, or tents using old tarps, mum's sheets; anything we could get our hands on, really. I remember having a blast building them and laughing uncontrollably with Tamby who loved to join in. She would try to burrow underneath to get to me and then jump on top of me, smothering me with wet sloppy kisses. Growing up with Tamby developed my lifelong love of dogs and blessed me with another three pups following her passing when I was fourteen. Tamby taught me unconditional love, what true joy felt like, how no one or nothing can greet you quite like a dog can, and to just enjoy each day. She was my buddy and companion for nearly fourteen years, and boy did we have some fun together. My heart warms every time I think of her and our adventures together growing up.

My other favourite memory was visiting my grandparents in New Zealand and having a blast swimming with my beloved Pop. He would often pretend to be a whale and spurt water up into the air - what fun we had together. Pop showed me true unconditional love, adventure, a love of the water and life in general. Sadly he passed away when I was nine and a half and I was devastated to lose him. I still clearly remember sitting in the church for his funeral and hearing the Minister say *"God has called Eddie up to heaven to join him,"* and instantly feeling anger rise within me.

How dare God take my beloved Pop away from me!

From that point on I felt strong animosity towards God, blaming him for taking my beloved Pop away. I mention this as I find it interesting the power of words on others, especially little children who don't know any better. This is a prime example of the effect one sentence had on my relationship with religion. The thought of church that followed that time in my life was, "It's bogus and takes away those I love. What's the point of going then?"

It brought up feelings of anger, disgust, hurt and betrayal. This continued through my childhood and into adulthood. I didn't step inside a church unless I had to for a funeral or wedding of very close family members or friends. Even then I remember feeling awkward, like I didn't belong and shouldn't be there. It was a weird feeling that wouldn't go away. I continued to harbour resentment well into later adulthood until sharing my story with a close friend who offered me this advice:

"Dianne, what if this was a lesson in learning about grief, and deepening your connection to God in doing so?"

I must admit I had honestly never thought about it in that way. Perhaps God (and religion) wasn't so bad after all? It still took me quite some time to process this and come to terms with my loss and deep-seated resentment towards what I felt was someone who had stolen my beloved Pop. I sat with that advice for many weeks, possibly months to allow it to sink deep into my heart. *Could I really see God in a more loving light?*

I am glad to say that God and I are back on good terms now.

For the most part, my childhood was happy. We enjoyed family trips to Shoal Bay or Port Macquarie each year, meeting new friends and awaiting the morning arrival of the Moove Man. Now I'm not sure if he was called the Moove Man, but I can vividly see him driving around the caravan park where we often stayed, in a small truck, beeping his horn to let everyone know he was there. Selling ice creams, yoghurt and moove milk - strawberry was my favourite, my sister loved chocolate. Simple pleasures, happy times that still bring a smile to my face and a warmth in my chest. My other favourite delight in Shoal Bay was the snow cones, shaved ice served in a cone-shaped piece of cardboard with flavouring squirted over the top of the ice. Delicious!

I was very lucky my parents took a lot of pictures of my sister and me growing up, so there are a lot of fond memories to look back on. I wonder at what point did that happy little girl (me) think she wasn't good enough or worthy of love, happiness, wealth, motherhood, success or healthy relationships? Early childhood is meant to be a time of exploration, wonderment, laughs, love, safety, kindness, and possibilities. Many things can impact this, some not so pleasant, and can alter the course of our life's path, leaving us uncertain about who we are (if we ever knew to begin with) and causing us to struggle at times to find ourselves again.

CHILDHOOD, RELATIONSHIPS & CAREER

My earliest memory of thinking such terrible thoughts was around 15 years old. I had a huge crush on this gorgeous, dark-haired, brown eyed boy named Beau. We regularly chatted on the phone, he would pass me notes in class, and I was totally hoping he would ask me to be his date at the Year 10 school formal. He didn't, but he did ask me to dance during the night. I remember coming home from the formal feeling elated he had done so. Ah, the bliss of teenage love (albeit unrequited).

The Christmas holiday period that followed saw me head to New Zealand for a couple of weeks to visit family. Excited to return home and speak to him, I heard nothing. No phone call, no returning my messages. So, I waited to see him once school went back in the new year. He would be my first heartache. I saw him chatting cosily with another girl in our year; she had blonde hair and blue eyes. I remember being quite curious and confused at first.

Maybe they were just friends? The next day I saw her wearing his jumper and my heart sank. They were more than just friends. People were now talking about them being a couple, and he pretty much blocked me. No more phone calls, notes, nothing at all. Like I no longer existed, or so I felt anyway. She was prettier than me, skinnier than I and therefore I decided she must be better than me. Men prefer blondes after all (or so I thought). That statement would haunt me for many more years before I realised it was all made up in my head.

A funny thing was that I internalised a lot of this and never really shared my thoughts with anyone. This became a recurring theme and statement throughout my childhood and adulthood.

I now realise how damaging this was to me and how much it affected my life. It wasn't until I went on the IVF journey that I was forced to look at and heal my deeper beliefs. From the outside, I seemed a confident child, girl, and woman, generally happy with life, albeit with the occasional mood swing (as we all have). Inside I felt empty, sad, confused, and longed for approval, love and validation from others. What a recipe for disaster, and to some degree it was, as much as it was a lesson in forgiveness, grace, compassion, advocacy and resilience. This led to unconscious weight loss, bordering on anorexia, where I felt disgusted with my body.

Why wasn't she enough, pleasing to the eye? Maybe if she was thinner life would be better?

I didn't even notice the weight loss, my mum did. See where the not;-enoughness comes from, maybe if I were X or Y, then Z. That poor woman was lost and my heart breaks for her looking back. All along she was always good enough and didn't need to change her physical appearance in the slightest.

Over the course of my late teens to early adulthood, I put on twenty-something kilos, waking up one morning and deciding this would need to change now. As the action-oriented person I am, I began my 'diet' and joined a gym, going there four times a week for cardio and weights. Within about six months, I had lost twenty-three kilos and felt elated at what a great job I had done. The funny thing was that when I looked in the mirror, I didn't see myself as thinner (and I most certainly was) and didn't dress any differently either. I still felt and saw the size fourteen woman in the mirror.

I have always seen myself as being different from my family, attributing it to being the black sheep of the family, feeling like I was on the outside and wishing for more closeness with them. Believing I looked different from them meant that I was, and that they saw it too. Isn't it so fascinating the way our minds work and influence our self-image. My relationship with my family was always distant, as I didn't let anyone get too close, while feeling alone and unfulfilled. My interactions with them were at a surface level, with little vulnerability on my part shared with them, nor any openness to connect deeply initiated by me.

A similar theme emerged during my career, where those same feelings of inadequacy, people pleasing, not being enough, and feeling worthless led me to be treated unfairly by a manager who knew exactly what she was doing and took great delight in seeing me fall apart. Constant snide remarks, denying me opportunities to progress my career and skill set, allocating me double, if not triple, the workload of my colleagues and the most challenging tasks assigned to me. The saddest part was that I never challenged them, believing they knew better than I did. After all, they were my manager, and perhaps I deserved to be treated poorly? I felt too scared to speak out or establish strong boundaries with them. What if they yelled at me? Or my workload got even higher? So I said nothing. This manager was also well-connected within the company's head office, and I truly believed at the time that no one would believe me even if I did say anything, so I remained miserable, afraid, and a mere shell of my former self. A number of years would pass before I would find the courage to move on from this position, and once I did I instantly felt free. I confided in a friend what I was experiencing and felt some relief in offloading.

The importance of finding your tribe cannot be underestimated. Having like-minded people around who inspire, nurture, support, and encourage you is invaluable, not to mention energising. Trust me, the emotional weight that was lifted was huge.

 JOURNAL PROMPT

Do you have a tribe that you can call on when needed as much as share your successes, joy and love?

Pattern of not good enough

I was literally breaking myself physically, mentally and emotionally and never recognised this until I couldn't function anymore. What do I mean? Think of lapses in memory, not retaining information just provided to you, difficulty in understanding, let alone completing simple tasks. Insomnia, complemented by food aversions, or not eating at all, and choosing to remain indoors on my own than be around others Life was just all too much to bear. I was a shell of my former self, miserable, alone and numb.

Thanks to therapy, a supportive and nurturing family friendship groups the tide began to turn and I began to see myself as whole, enough and an asset - for the very first time in my life. This was quite unnerving at first, as I struggled to get comfortable with feeling uncomfortable.

I allowed myself to cry and do so deeply. Once I started I found I couldn't stop, the tears kept flowing. I knew something wasn't right and wasn't sure what to do to fix things.

March 2016, I rang my GP and arranged for a mental health care plan that would allow me to access professional counselling to deal with my anxiety, fears, hurt, trauma and whatever else reared its head during the process. Thankfully this was before I began my IVF journey, but it was something I desperately wanted to 'fix'.

I am proud to say those pieces have now been reconfigured in a way that feels aligned, pure, calm, loving and whole. There were so many lessons learnt in the aftermath of the trauma, most significantly around how much I gave my power away to others and still felt miserable. Such a contradiction! I wanted others to make me feel better about myself and that didn't happen. I made that mean I wasn't a good person. How completely wrong was I.

Over the course of my career I have always done well, working my way up the ranks from staff member, to manager, assessor and quality assurer. I loved each step of the way and learned so much about working with differing personalities and experience, which enabled me to draw on this skillset as I changed jobs. I have always loved working with and supporting others as best as I could. I disliked seeing others down or feeling lost, and often jumped right in to help without even being asked, sometimes, my people pleasing tendencies were in full swing.

During my early twenties I spent three years working in the UK, initially under a short-term contract in a public school. I was later rewarded with a long-term stint; an eighteen month contract, right up until I returned home to Australia. Hard work equated to recognition and reward for me back then and somewhere along the line this became distorted to the point of burnout and overwhelm.

Can you see the common theme of not learning from or acknowledging my achievements and successes? I never expected them to happen, or gave myself any credit for getting there. I felt like it all came down to luck, not that I was particularly skilled at what I did; people related well to and respected me and my professional opinion and support. It's as if I disassociated from life, both in terms of my role in it and my own active participation in it.

At the time of my breakthrough, I was in a toxic romantic relationship and relentlessly overworked, before finally escaping to another team that showed me nothing but love, kindness, and compassion. The feeling that I was failing and a burden on the team remained strong, but this team and my manager at the time really saved me. I am not sure they ever knew how much they provided me a safe space to be me, and learn without being belittled or ostracised. They were the ones who supported me in taking the time to decompress and begin the healing process. I will never forget their kindness and remain in contact with them today. The difference between these two work experiences is opposite, and yet both had a profound influence on my life. It all came down to the environment I created for myself and the people around me.

CHILDHOOD, RELATIONSHIPS & CAREER

Here's just a taster of the relationships I have learnt and grown from (thank goodness). Heeding advice I should have given myself at the time, if any of these resonate with you in any way, don't be too hard on yourself. We are all human and imperfectly perfect as we are.

All of us are just doing the best with what we have at the time. Be gentle, give yourself grace and most of all be kind to you. These are the most influential relationships that have shaped me, not that there were a gazillion of them, but I do believe it is important to be transparent about where I am now and what led me here. They formed a part of my journey, albeit a heartbreaking one at the time. So, in no particular order, here goes:

Guy One was in his late forties, and I was in my early forties, and he ignored me unless I messaged him or met up when it was convenient for him. This lasted for around seven months, and despite some protests and requests for him to consider my needs and availability (he would at times cancel at the last minute to do overtime - money was very important to him), he would only think of himself and his son. It seemed like I was speaking another language to him, or he just didn't want to hear me out. I feel the latter is the correct answer. I didn't find him attractive, except that he had a teenage son and was very close to him. To me this seemed like I had my fantasy of a ready-made family walk in. I remember one incident when we had made plans to spend the weekend together and the day before he cancelled, telling me he had picked up extra shifts that would see his rake in an extra $2000. I reminded him of our plans and his response was "Don't you realise how much money I can bring in?"

Umm, yes I could. How about talking about it first rather than just cancelling already confirmed plans?

We had been dating around five months by this stage. Nothing, no consideration, apology, nothing. And so he worked, while I stewed, and I saw him the following weekend. Why Dianne, you ask? Pretty reasonable question. Why didn't I just dump his sorry ass? I didn't want him to leave me; that instilled such overwhelming fear I would have done anything to ensure it didn't happen. Fear-avoidant attachment example number one.

He wasn't much of a conversationalist unless the topic interested him, and he preferred messaging over phone calls to communicate (big red flag in hindsight!). In the end, he just stopped messaging one day, and I stopped trying to get his attention, all the while wondering what I had done wrong and what was wrong with me. The simple answer was that I did nothing wrong; he was the wrong guy for me.

Guy Two was too interested in sowing his wild oats to commit to anything serious, and also stopped messaging one day. He was in his early twenties (as I was) and a party animal, loving nothing more than going out to dance and listen to music. He had the most gorgeous green eyes and olive complexion, and that smile... He knew it too, cheeky bugger! He was confident, fun, easy on the eye and sexy as hell (or so I thought). I was elated when he noticed me and came up to me on the dance floor. He had chosen me, this gorgeous male, not any other girl that night, he had chosen me. Gosh I am such a romantic at heart! Things fizzled out as quickly as they had begun. Years later I saw him on a group tour to Pamplona, he smiled and walked away to spend time with another girl.

Guy Three wanted to have fun only; he even told me so, and I fell in love with the idea of being in love with him. You can guess how that ended three years later. Yep, I know I should have known better. When I look back on that time, the thrill excited me; he was easy on the eye and sounded like a great dad and family man (ding ding! These were the qualities I was looking for in a partner). When I look back on that time, I worked around his availability, which was often very early in the morning or immediately after work. Never anywhere he could be seen with me and communicating only via the Kik app, where messages are deleted the same day.

You would think that that on its own would have been a big red flag, but nope! I wanted him to want me, not just physically, but emotionally too. And that's where he and I differed; he wasn't after an emotional connection, just a physical one. Again, I believed that if I gave him what he wanted, then he would like me beyond a physical relationship. The fantasy of being in love with being in love was incredibly strong and had such power over me.

Guy Four did the most damage to my self-image, wooing me in the beginning and introducing me to his son very early on (a big mistake!). When he realised that he had me, which was pretty early on, the sweet words and flattery were soon replaced with subtle digs and insults, which only served to reinforce that I wasn't good enough and deserved to be treated in such a way (wrong!). He even used his young son to deliver snide comments (he was way too young to understand nor know any better) and suggested we spend less time together and only visit when he asked me to. I remember being ecstatic when asked to pick up his son from daycare, feeling we were a family unit now, when in reality, all I was was a convenience. The messages he sent me hurt more and more as time went on, and I remained silent, choosing not to stand up for myself or pull him into line for disrespecting me. I believed that if I just pushed through and saw things out, he would change and choose a life with me. He didn't.

I never saw it at the time, the culmination of him and a toxic workspace was the eventual breaking of me, literally. I was spent emotionally, mentally, physically and psychologically. Crying endlessly every day, not sleeping, not eating or eating poorly was just the tip of the iceberg.

Now I hear you ask, Dianne, what the hell were you doing? I know, I know. Gosh if this was a girlfriend telling me this was how she was being treated I would have told her to hot tail it out of there and not look back. And yet I stayed and stayed and stayed.

I stayed because he was the ready made family I so longed for myself. I stayed because I saw him as a good father (and I wanted a child of my own). I stayed because I believed at the time if I gave my all it would be enough and he'd love me. I stayed because I was embarrassed to tell anyone why we would have split up and judged for being stupid, naive or difficult.

I stayed because I didn't know any better (I truly believed I deserved to be treated this way in order to be loved).

Around the same time, I was also battling a manager who enjoyed her own subtle digs and allocating a two- to three-person workload to me to complete on my own. At the time, I didn't really think much of either relationship and how wrong they were to me. I was just trying to stay afloat, afraid that if I permitted myself to open up the floodgate to my emotions, it would be so overwhelming that I would never recover. Crying most days (keeping this to myself) and sharing only with one close girlfriend the extent of my struggles with said manager. I tried harder every day to be the good girl, the best employee. I tried not to show how much they repeatedly hurt me. I continually tried to rise to their challenges, whatever they wanted. It was never enough and it was never going to be; that was the whole point. It was like they had some perverse pleasure in watching me suffer (and they both knew I did). Sure they never saw me cry, but they did see the bags under my eyes from lack of sleep, the weight loss, an ever-growing quiet demeanour, and slowly withdrawing from those around me.

Said romantic relationship thankfully only lasted six months, but the damage done in that time took me years of therapy to recover and heal from. I came to realise the notion of giving my power away, and I certainly did with him 1000%.

I am embarrassed to say that I allowed him to treat and speak to me so poorly. Eyeing me up and down with a disapproving look after coming back from holidays and indulging in a few too many sweet delights (this showed in my hips). I have never worn a bikini again. I allowed him to have digs at me via text messages, and instead of replying in kind or calling him out on it, I felt defeated and hurt at why he would choose to do so in the first place. And I said nothing, but felt everyone.

It finally ended with him moving away, under the pretence of just for a couple of weeks, then not even a week later, telling me he was driving six hours away for good. My heart broke and I burst into tears. His response was silence, and I hung up so I could calm down. What a douchebag! He didn't even bother to call me the next morning to check I was ok. In fact, he had the nerve to message me the next afternoon with a random message about getting his lawns mowed. Like what! So, despite him moving six hours away and telling me he was staying there, he was still playing games with me and using his young son to do so.

The relief when I finally cut the imaginary cord to him was huge. Such a big weight was lifted, and I felt free. Mind you, this took a couple of years, following therapy, distance, support from friends, and time.

So why am I sharing these stories, you ask? And rightly so. We all have stories that make up the fabric of our lives, each different and unique in its way. Who we are today is a result of who we were yesterday, and who we are choosing to be tomorrow. My past thoughts, behaviours, actions and beliefs have all shaped who I was in each of those moments - good, bad or ugly. For as long as I can remember I have wanted to be a mum, carrying and birthing a beautiful healthy bub of my own. That's the dream right. Yet it seemed to elude me, year after year after year. It felt such a deep longing in my heart, soul, every fibre of my being really I just couldn't imagine not being a mum. That literally felt like my heart breaking at such a thought.

What point am I trying to get to here? Well, my point is that there is such a strong connection between my self image, my longing to be a mum, my career and my less than desirable relationships.
Throughout my career, I believed I could help others and be the champion for those who didn't have anyone to speak up for them.

I believed in my relationships I could save them from the life they were living and replace it with my fantasy of a white picket fence loving family unit.
I believed that being a mum would complete me and my life would be whole.

I believed there was no reason I couldn't have it all.

It wouldn't be until I began to work on healing my self-image that my desire to be a mum would be realised.

Now, it wasn't just my romantic relationships that had a significant impact; my social relationships were just as impactful, if not even more so. I was not the kind of girl who had a gazillion girlfriends; I was the one who pretty much kept to myself and had a few close friends during school and university, branching further afield once I began working and later moving overseas to live for three years. Even still, I often kept my cards close to my chest and never divulged my deepest fears and desires, let alone when I was feeling hurt or sad. To me these were a sign of weakness and undesirable. In reality they show I am human like everyone else on the planet and imperfectly perfect.

There were a couple of friends who had a profound impact on me, both positively and not so positively. Either way they were some steep learning curves that taught me alot about myself and how I interact with them and the world in general.

The first one was a long term friend, having met at primary school. We floated in and out of each other's lives before solidifying our friendship when she had her first child, just as I had returned from three years of living and working in Birmingham, England. UK. From there, we spent a lot of time together, me helping her with her son and going clubbing when his dad had him for the weekend. Our friendship was always quite complex, with me earning a good income and her earning much less than mine. I say 'complex' because there were many times when a divide existed between what I could afford to do and what she could, which was neither our fault, but rather the circumstances we were living with at the time. She relied heavily on me as her source of support, comfort, and companionship, which I was more than happy to offer most of the time. Where I found it tricky was when she saw no need to help herself and expected it to be done for her. I am by no means suggesting she shouldn't have received help, as there are and were times I needed help. For me I struggled with this belief in areas when no one could help, that it was entirely up to her to make it possible. And when help was received it was expected rather than appreciated.

Our friendship eventually reached a point where I felt it was heavily one-sided and my issues, problems or difficulties no longer mattered. I felt seen but not heard and really struggled with this to be honest. I was and still am to some degree a people pleaser and wondered when I might receive some support, and didn't feel I was asking much to get it.

It ended after an insignificant conversation where I was talking out some heavy emotional issues within myself while she vacuumed around me, every now and then looking at me and nodding. I was devastated to say the least. It did not matter what I had to say, or that I was on the verge of tears. At that moment I decided it did matter to me, and I told her so. She shrugged her shoulders and continued vacuuming. I left and never returned. That was a key moment in setting boundaries both with myself and others. I completely understand that we all have a lot going on in our lives, and if you expect me to listen and support, I don't feel it is too much to ask for the same in return. Is it?

Another friend has always had the very best of intentions and has the biggest heart. They push me to do better and reach my full potential which was fantastic, except for the timing of it all. At the time I was falling apart and barely keeping it together mentally or emotionally. I just wasn't capable of being my best let alone expanding out into unknown territory - that was more fear I just didn't need to deal with; I had enough of it already to manage. However, I never said no, I don't want to, or it's too much right now, thinking that they knew best. In some ways they did, in others not so much. What I desperately needed was time to decompress, process and heal before making any big moves. I did end up taking extended time off work, which unfortunately wasn't used as best as it could have been. Again, I felt she knew best how to spend this time off; in reality, I could have used it much better for myself. We did enjoy many travels together and exploring style both in my wardrobe and home environment. It opened my eyes up to new ways of seeing and thinking which was awesome.

What I learnt from her was the importance of speaking up without hiding behind the fear of an argument ensuing; the importance of setting boundaries both with myself and others, and being ok with them not liking it; that I do know who I am, what I want and don't need to rely so heavily on others for this; that some things don't last forever and that's ok it doesn't mean something is wrong.

Having very different personalities, there were clashes, arguments, tears, periods of silence and distance for a while. Looking back, this was another instance of me giving my power away in full, while at the same time knowing that a lot of what was discussed and done was not right for me. I felt it and ignored my intuition - don't be like me in that way! I am proud to say we are still friends today and she has been one of my biggest champions and someone I am proud to have by my side.

Another was a work colleague with whom I clicked from the get-go. Have you ever met someone, and it just seems right?

They inspire, motivate, challenge and support you and vice versa. You feel your most confident and comfortable around them and feel safe to be your most vulnerable. This was them, both of us wanting a more fulfilling and expansive life while also healing some pretty heavy trauma and toxic habits. I have enjoyed many heartfelt discussions with her on relationships, food, money, energy, communication, and the list goes on.

She inspires me to be my best self while also keeping me grounded by holding me to account when I get a bit too much (as I am sure we all do). She has taught me compassion for myself, resilience, and inspired me to expand my self-image and what I see myself as being capable of, and has created a safe space for me to be vulnerable. I am proud to call her one of my closest friends and know we will continue to grow and expand our lives to the fullest potential.

My most recent friendship is with another amazing human who has the biggest heart in spite of many health and personal challenges being thrown her way. She has a go-getter attitude while also prioritising her self care (especially mentally and emotionally) which is such an inspiring role model for her children. She is only ever a phone call away and one of the first to ask if I am ok and do I need anything (despite having a lot on her own plate most days). I feel inspired, energised and happy in her presence and believe she will be a positive role model for my precious E as he/she grows. We met online and hit it off from the get-go. She is brash, kind, open, creative, and most importantly real in who she is.

Now these aren't my only friendships, they are the ones who have had quite a significant impact on my life and self-image.

They have challenged, inspired, motivated, depleted, scared and grown me.

 **REFLECTION**

Are you in the best surroundings for you?
Does it uplift, encourage, nurture and grow you?
What about the people you surround yourself with?
How do you feel when you are around them?
Does it feel light, calm, free and energising? Or is it heavy, tiring and just plain blah?

I invite you to take time to really think deeply on these questions. The difference in who you surround yourself with and where you place yourself can greatly impact not only yourself but your life, yes it makes that big a difference. I can't begin to tell you how much.

What I will say is please think about it and decide if it is or isn't working for you, what small steps can you tackle right now to start actioning a change towards the life and tribe you truly are seeking. What qualities do they hold, what are they doing/ being? Where might you find them?

Thinking about my early days - my childhood and career, I realise how little I actually thought of myself.

Thoughts that came to my mind included:
- You are worthless
- You are not enough
- You are a failure
- No one wants, loves or likes you
- You have to do more to get people to like you, what you are doing isn't enough
- You are ugly
- You are not skinny enough
- You are not pretty enough
- You are just not enough

This was not the fun kind of realisation either. It was sad and heavy. What a way to see myself, but that was exactly how I did see myself. The picture I had of myself was a dismal one at best, and it was a heavy weight to carry around. Not a physical weight, this was a suffocating emotional weight. The emotional weight felt so much heavier to bear. This was not how I wanted to see myself nor live my life, things had to change. Life was not worth living if it meant feeling miserable, lost and lonely.

But how would I even go about this?

Was it even possible for me? Maybe this was how life was meant to play around for me.

REFLECTION

1. How do you see yourself, does any of this hit home?
2. Do you believe these thoughts can change and support you to lead a fulfilling, joyous and satisfying life? I must admit I never thought it could, that life was a predestined path I had no control or influence over. Boy was I wrong and as I discovered much later, pleasantly so.
3. What do you believe about motherhood, love, money, life? Do you believe it is or can be in abundance for you?

I didn't and can't help but wonder how much impact this had on my past cycles and life in general.

CHAPTER 2

Relationships

"How you love yourself is how you teach others to love you,"

– RUPI KAUR

Such a simple statement isn't it? In reality, how many of us embody it? I know I never did. Why on earth would I devote time to loving myself? Isn't that a bit selfish, snobbish or egotistical? I could just imagine what everyone would think of me if I did

Dianne's a self-centred witch, too obsessed with herself to be bothered with anyone else. Who does she think she is anyway? She's nothing special and needs to stop pretending to be.

These negative thoughts would rear their ugly head whenever I would try to think of a way to behave differently - like rejoining online dating, setting up my own business so I could step away from corporate life where I currently worked or even something so simple as saying 'no' to something I didn't want to do. The last one was extremely difficult for me to do. What if the other person was upset with me, or worse, yelled at me or stopped speaking to me? That was too scary to bear. But what about what I wanted? Did that even matter?

I don't know about you but the endless negative chatter in my mind was physically draining on its own let alone the emotional rollercoaster I was on. It still amazes me how poorly many of us (me included) treat and speak to ourselves, when we would never do so to our children, family or friends. I know it has always been there but it seemed to be really loud when looking for ways to set up my own wellness and wellbeing business. *How could I do this when I wasn't taking care of myself? Isn't that a bit hypocritical?*

I wanted out of corporate life, out of the life I was living, and to jump straight into the life and love of my dreams.

How would I even go about it anyway? What does loving yourself even mean?

Just thinking of this back then was incredibly overwhelming, anxiety-inducing and scary. Thoughts automatically went to celebrities who had lots of money to do as they pleased. This wasn't me. Yes I was on a good wage but I certainly wasn't a multi-millionaire!

When I think back on my life, taking care of myself wasn't the 'done' thing. It was better (or so I thought) to care for others first. Plus I believed if I did so, that would earn me their love and affection. The issue evolved into whatever I did was never enough or worthy. It was because they simply weren't interested (it had nothing to do with who I was as a person or how attractive I was). So, I kept pushing and maintaining consistent habits, hoping for a different outcome, which of course never came.

I believed (as many of us do) that love came from others and it had to be earned (whatever that looked like). For me, that looked like giving and doing for my partner whatever I felt I *'should'* without any thought for myself and whether it felt ok for me to do so. One partner, Grant, initiated contact via a dating app and was very complimentary in the beginning. It felt great to feel wanted and desired by a man. He fit the mould of what I was looking for - an instant family. What I didn't notice at first was he drove a two-seater van (not family-friendly) and lived in a small two-bedroom apartment (no room for another child). I ignored both red flags.

Once we had begun seeing each other in person he, his son and I went away for his birthday. I was elated and felt this was a big step in our relationship. Now I had not long returned from a month overseas enjoying delicious food and shopping. No counting calories, just enjoying tasty meals, drinks and snacks. We visited a waterpark for his birthday and I was wearing a bikini. Standing at the top of a slide I felt his eyes on me, looking me up and down, stopping at my eyes and feeling embarrassed and ashamed. He looked at me with disdain, turned and joined his son on the waterslide. My hand instantly went to my waist trying to cover it. I felt ugly, fat and unattractive to him, I followed them down the water slide and walked behind them in silence, quickly grabbing my coverall to hide my body. Nothing was said between him and I, but it did set a course for his son to later call me 'hippo,' which I am sure his father taught him to say.

That hurt, deeply. I was far from overweight and yet felt like I was. What hurt the most was when I would ask his son not to speak to me that way, Grant glanced at me and asked his son to stop. But it didn't stop. I felt like he was only placating me by speaking with his son. I believe Grant was the initiator. His son was only five, and didn't know better. Why would he behave so disrespectfully and intentionally cause hurt?

I was chasing him rather than letting him chase me, holding out for one day when he might show me even a glimmer of the love that I was searching for.

Sure, we've all been there with unrequited love and chasing what doesn't want or is meant for us. I know that a part of our life's path is to learn what does and doesn't serve us, and make decisions from there. Now, this wasn't every relationship, but it was a common occurrence throughout many of them, one much worse than the others. I admit I was a follower, believing that 'they' (friends and partners) knew better than I did in terms of how they dressed, ate, what they did and when, who they spent time with, and who they didn't.

They were chasing after their desires and following their interests and curiosities, and I wasn't. They realised their dreams of marriage and family, and I didn't. On the outside they thought I had the life, travelling whenever and wherever I wanted (which was awesome and I highly recommend you delight in the travel bug if it does tickle your fancy). People told me I had the life; that I was better off without the responsibility of kids, or the hassle of a partner. At the time I shrugged off their comments, not really taking any notice. In reality, they were one hundred percent wrong, that was exactly what I wanted, and I used travel as a means of distraction from focusing on my hearts' true desires.

Don't get me wrong, the travel adventures I had over the past twenty-odd years have been amazing! Blessed with the income to do so, I was able to explore Europe, America, Asia and the United Kingdom. But having this as my sole focus led me to reach forty, single and childless, and very unhappy with life. Travel blessed me with independence, career growth, cultural expansion, and food delights. Yet, deep inside, I always felt shy, awkward, an outsider, and alone.

Believing that I wasn't enough or worthy impacted many of my friendships and all of my romantic relationships. It was tricky for people to get to know me and as was often the case, people moved on. They knew the surface layer to me, which was robotic, uninteresting, unopinionated and blah. No fault on their part,

I didn't exactly make it easy for them. With potential partners, I predominantly did the chasing, desperately trying to gain their attention and affections, which of course I never truly did. And it hurt, badly, and deeply, severely damaging my self image even further. I allowed them to disrespect me, ignore me, insult me, belittle me, and ultimately abandon me. This version of me was so full of shame, disgust with herself, a scarcity mindset, and desperately seeking others' approval and validation. I say a scarcity mindset as I obsessed over what I believed I was lacking. In my case this was time, money, love, health, connection and belonging.

I handed my power over to others completely, not even a little bit, but fully. Their opinion and treatment of me solely determined how I saw myself which was not in a positive light in the slightest.

My hair was too frizzy. I wasn't blonde. I wasn't thin enough, toned enough or tanned enough. My nose was too pointy. I had too much cellulite. My varicose veins were unattractive. My lips were too small as were my eyes. I had a double chin. My tummy had loose skin. My eyes weren't blue. I wasn't sporty. I didn't dress in provocative clothing.

This was just the tip of the iceberg of the thoughts constantly running through my head about myself. Perhaps I was harsher on me than they ever were? In part I can also see why they were not interested, as I hardly showed up as my best and most confident self. I remember being the girl who stood in the corner, afraid of being noticed, not wanting to be the centre of attention. Not maintaining eye contact and turning my body away when anyone remotely attractive walked past. Surely they couldn't be interested in me.

No wonder I remained single for a lot of my adulthood. So afraid to be with anyone for fear of being hurt or abandoned by them, and afraid I would forever remain alone. The issue of abandonment is an interesting one for me. It has been a common issue that keeps rearing its ugly head, and certainly resurfaced during my IVF cycles. I am a little confused as to why, I don't ever remember being left as a kid and having a good upbringing in a stable home. Yet it has had such a powerful effect on me and my relationships. The fear behind it was so strong at times it was literally paralysing. It drove me to drop everything I was doing when my partners called, allowing them to dictate what we did and when, scheduling my plans around them, giving my all when they gave me very little of themselves. Quite sad, hey...

* * * * *

Family relationships

I am the eldest of two kids living life in suburban Sydney. For as long as I can remember, I saw myself as the black sheep of my family. I felt different to everyone else, and so I kept those dearest to me at a distance. I always wanted the closeness I observed in my friends with their families and didn't seem to have with mine. Now I admit that lies with me as I had a choice throughout my life to change that, albeit I was completely unsure how to do so until recently, let alone aware that I even felt this way. I just thought I was a loner and that was how my life was meant to be. Could it have been shyness instead perhaps? All I knew was I felt an uneasiness in my body and didn't know why. I would sit at the end of tables or at the back of rooms, during large gatherings so as not to be noticed or stand out in any way. My posture was hunched, head down and I avoided eye contact. I felt awkward if I am honest, awful in my body, style and personality.

I have always felt closest to my dad while my sister was closest to our mum. I guess most kids naturally gravitate to certain people. I was the tomboy, busy playing outside with the boys next door, my dog and 'helping' Dad in the garden. Full disclosure, when I say 'helping' I mean digging up plants, hosing the fence and him, or flicking the pebbles in our front driveway with my feet while sitting in my rocker as a baby. All innocent fun and memories he still laughs at today. With my extended family, I feel closest to my elder cousin (we are less than 12 months apart in age), as he shares similar beliefs with me, a sense of humour, and life goals. We all spent a lot of time together growing up, congregating at my paternal grandparents' house. Their place was always full of love, laughs, great food and such a strong connection. I remember it as a warm, inviting second home that I still feel fondly towards and miss dearly. Sadly both my paternal grandparents have passed on and I am blessed and so grateful for many memories of our time spent together.

Funny how I often felt like an outsider and never quite belonging anywhere even with being blessed with a loving family. I now realise this was all down to my thoughts and beliefs at the time that I skewed based on misunderstanding, naivety and innocence of childhood. The desire to belong and have meaningful connections was strong all throughout my life.

> **REFLECTION**
>
> *Have you ever stopped to look at your relationships and whether they align with you or not? And if not, what would you like them to be and can do about it?*

CHAPTER 3

Road to Motherhood

"The moment a child is born, the mother is also born. She never existed before. The woman existed, but the mother, never. A mother is something absolutely new,"

– UNKNOWN

ROAD TO MOTHERHOOD

Gosh what a road I have travelled, with so many twists and turns, roadblocks, U-turns and time spent in the breakdown lane. Whoever wrote the above quote described motherhood to perfection. I knew that a whole new version of me would be born and life we never be the same. How did I get here you ask?

I celebrated my fortieth year travelling around New Zealand, America and the Mediterranean. What a way to celebrate! The following year was a quieter one that really got me thinking about babies, how much I wanted to be a mum and at the same time feeling unworthy, not good enough and that maybe my body was failing me for not having become a mum yet.

In Chapter 1, I shared a little about freezing my eggs aged 43 years old. At the time it was a task to complete on the checklist of becoming a mum. In reality it was a big deal, intrusive on my body and in some ways a little too late to be doing that only to then sit back a few more years before using them (for me anyway). As I said in the beginning, this is my story and mine alone and by no means, is it the right way for anyone other than me. I look back now and wonder why Dr Adrian didn't advise me against freezing my eggs if I was then not going to use them for another two to three years down the track. Better still why not tell me that it would have been better to do a full cycle (egg collection, fertilisation and embryo transfer) and try for a baby back then? Yes, IVF is a time and numbers game, but it is also an age game and age was most definitely not on my side. Nonetheless the choice was mine, albeit an uninformed one and it would be three years later before I would realise just how big of a deal it truly was.

My advice to my younger self and to you (if you are younger than me) is to consider what you see for your future and if motherhood is in fact a part of it. If so, perhaps consider whether freezing your eggs at the age you are now, might be an option for you to access later on when you are ready. You are more resilient than you give yourself credit for and it is mostly certainly not stubbornness asking for and going after what you want. It's called having your own back and aligning your actions with your true desires.

Now there are no certainties in the world of IVF, and the research clearly shows the younger you do so, the higher quality the eggs are likely to be, which may then lead to a higher rate of success. Again nothing is guaranteed, but it might be something worth exploring now.

I am not knocking my doctor, nor anyone else who chooses to freeze their eggs as I did at age 43. In hindsight I would say to the younger me to consider their decisions and whether waiting even longer to then use them was the wisest decision to make. If I could be teleported back in time, I wonder if I would do things differently. Prior to falling pregnant and having Eva, I would have automatically answered yes, nothing like the benefit of hindsight. Now that I am blessed with her in my life, I am not so sure. To change the past would mean I am changing the future and the thought of not having Eva in my future is heartbreaking. So, that question is no longer so black and white, and instead taking it all on board as life lessons means that I have gained incredible wisdom, insight, compassion for myself and others, and a truly understanding of the importance of self-advocacy, more than I ever had before. Life seems to have a way of turning out exactly as it is meant to (even if not the path we thought or wanted to take). I didn't know it at the time, but I guess my unwavering belief and desire to become a mum, saw it become reality in the most loving way possible for me (and Eva).

Back to the start of 2020, during the COVID 19 pandemic, which saw the initial statewide cancellation and then subsequent resumption of IVF cycles. What a relief! Thankfully the statewide IVF cancellation wasn't as long as everyone (including me) first thought and I was able to try again with a new doctor. I. was positive this time it would be successful.

I met my new specialist, where we reviewed my medical history including my last cycle, followed by a series of blood tests to get a baseline and begin my first (of what would end up being four) fresh egg collection cycles. Throughout those four cycles I would experience multiple chemical pregnancies, a miscarriage, average size and quality eggs collected, pregnancy symptoms each cycle, none of which resulted in a lasting pregnancy. What was consistent throughout the cycles was me being told my eggs were the problem and I should just move to donor conception. I guess from the doctors' perspective he was trying to save me time, money and heartache. What I think he failed to see was that moving from the choice to use my own eggs to using a donor is deeply personal and fraught with guilt, shame, insecurity and particularly in my case I wasn't ready to go down that path at that time. I remember saying to myself often, *"Dianne, I am betting on you, I have confidence that we can do this!"*. My heart was telling me to continue trying to use my own eggs.

The first two cycles were pretty similar. We collected four average quality eggs that were good sizes and suitable to progress to the fertilisation stage. All four eggs were fertilised and subsequently created two embryos that would develop over the coming days and be viable for implantation. For me, that meant I had two embryos implanted for each of the first two cycles. The reason for doing so was to increase my chance of successful implantation and pregnancy. For each cycle, I did feel the sharp, strong implantation cramps followed by waves of nausea, tender breasts, headaches and fatigue. Following the embryo transfer, I was asked to take a few injections to increase progesterone levels, designed to aid implantation. In my case, roughly three days following my last injection during the two week wait, so that's roughly day five in the two week wait, I noticed the pregnancy symptoms disappear overnight (literally). Still no period two weeks later, and confirmed chemical pregnancies. Disappointed and heartbroken to say the least, you have to give me credit for being a trooper (or stubbornly determined) to continue.

So two cycles down and those closest to me were getting concerned this might not work and how I would cope with that (fair question to ask). Considering the toll it was taking on my body and age, it was fair to consider whether continuing was the wisest decision for me. When I say it took a toll on my body, for me that meant my blood pressure dropped after each egg collection and embryo transfer. I am not sure if it was nerves or a response to the anaesthetic, possibly both.

Nonetheless as each cycle passed, the drop was more significant and often it took me a longer recovery time each round. Funny what we are happy to put our bodies through when we want something so badly, isn't it?

Each time my blood pressure would drop quite a lot and I'd start to feel nauseous. I would then receive medication to fix both issues and have a saline IV afterwards for about forty minutes before I was allowed to go home. Mind you, this was combined with strong stomach cramps following the egg collection procedure, with a heat pack and some Panadol slightly easing it. I would then head home to sleep and rest for the rest of the day. Often this would continue until the following day when I would wake feeling washed out and fatigued. By day three, I was feeling about ninety per cent back to normal and would resume work activities. I should disclose that for each cycle I chose and was blessed with support from my work to take off both the day of and the following day for all of my procedures.

So on top of undergoing multiple cycles, I did three back-to-back cycles (many others have done a lot more back-to-back cycles than me) which was a lot looking back. I say a lot as it must have taken an incredible toll on my body, continuously pumping it full of medications, supplements, acupuncture needles, let alone blood tests, and internal ultrasounds.

Choosing to undergo back to back cycles was always my choice and one that I own completely. Both the doctor and nursing staff were helpful in offering me options after each unsuccessful cycle all the while indicating my chances of success may be improved by undergoing back-to-back cycles as my body was already geared up for it. In some ways, this does make sense. In another way taking a break and allowing my body to decompress from such big events was perhaps a better move. Ahh... the benefit of hindsight! I also can't help but wonder if the suggestion to do back-to-back cycles is financially motivated by fertility clinics. Not that I am accusing them of any impropriety, but it does leave me wondering.

The third cycle

April 2021, my third cycle resulted in a very painful miscarriage. I say painful as it was both physically and emotionally. Physically, it felt like I was passing a brick, my whole body tightening in pain, my back arching and my face contorted as my beloved embryos passed through me in the shower. All that was left of them were two bloodied blobs on my shower floor. I stood looking at them, crying, noticing one looked bigger than the other. Emotionally it was a whole other heaviness that left me feeling like I was suffocating in sadness, frustration and disappointment. No one understood what I was going through - they probably did but in all honesty, I wasn't open to hearing others' experiences. I was hurting and longed to be comforted, to be told everything would be ok. That I would be ok. Except I felt that I wouldn't and didn't know how to comfort myself, and so I didn't. I cried in the shower, withdrew from everyone and spent time on my own.

By June 2021 I was still feeling off, nothing I could quite put my finger on, but something in my body didn't feel right. I wanted someone to tell me what was going on, since I didn't know myself. I decided to schedule a telehealth with my GP. Luckily I had been with my GP for over twenty years, and he knew me well. Describing my symptoms to him - constant fatigue, a heaviness in my stomach not gluten-related, just feeling off overall. I knew these weren't particularly descriptive symptoms. He suggested I see an obstetrician to check that there were no remnants left in my body following my miscarriage. I hadn't even thought of that, now I was worried something was really wrong. Surprised I could get an appointment so quickly I felt somewhat relieved that I could get answers soon.

I met with Dr Harry feeling calm in his presence, our consultation went like this:

Dr Harry: "So tell me Dianne, why are you here today?"

Me: "I had a miscarriage following my third IVF cycle in April 2021. I passed two blood clots, one large, one small, in the shower. Since then my body has felt off. My GP suggested I come to see you".

Dr Harry: "OK I am glad you have come to see me. Can you tell me a little about your IVF cycles and the outcomes of each?"

Me: "Sure, I have completed three cycles using my own eggs to date. For all three cycles I had two embryos implanted. The first two cycles resulted in chemical pregnancies and in my most recent cycle I miscarried."

Dr Harry: "OK thanks for letting me know, that must have been painful and heartbreaking for you. Let's see what I can do to help."

Me: "Thank you."

Dr Harry: "OK so first of all I think we need to arrange a dilation and curettage, hysteroscopy, laparoscopy and clean out your fallopian tubes. Just to make sure nothing is left in our body from the chemical pregnancies and miscarriage. Clean everything out so if you are going to do another cycle it's a fresh start for your body. How does that sound?"

Me: "Gosh, ok. That sounds big but good."

Dr Harry: "Great. I can schedule you in once you have menstruated. How long is your cycle and where are you at in your current menstrual cycle."

Me: "I am due to bleed in about one week, my cycle is usually a twenty-eight day cycle."

Dr Harry: "Ok thanks for that, I think we'll schedule you in then for two weeks' time, you'll be in for probably two to three days, and we'll go from there. How does that sound?"

Me: "Sounds good"

I added the date into my calendar, hopeful this would help with future IVF cycles.

* * * * *

My dad drove me to the hospital for my scheduled procedures. I checked in and was escorted to the pre op area and dressed ready for surgery. It all happened pretty quickly and before I knew it, I was waking up in the recovery room. The pain was extreme for me and I have a high pain threshold. The nurse beside me showed me where I could administer more pain relief as I needed it, while also not giving me too much. I must have clicked the 'magic' button quite a few times and then finally felt a wave of relief and the pain easing.

I must have fallen back asleep, as I woke up in a private hospital room and saw Mum and Dad sitting opposite me. Feeling a little groggy and nauseous, I felt like I had been run over by a truck. Everything felt sore, and it was really uncomfortable to cough or move, so I tried to lay as still as I could. Mum had brought me some gluten-free ginger nut biscuits which were perfect to ease the nausea. I am not sure how much time had passed but the nurse brought in my dinner: chicken curry. This was not what I was expecting to eat after surgery and the smell of the curry made my nausea worse. I was hungry from not eating much all day so I took a mouthful. *It couldn't be that bad could it?*

Yep, it was worse than I could have imagined. Not even swallowing the first bite I felt the nausea rise up my throat, genuinely worried I was going to throw up. Dad noticed my facial expression and grabbed a sick bag just in time. Up came the chicken curry. Thankfully another nurse arrived to check in on me as I was sick. She took one look at my meal and said, "You definitely shouldn't be having this. I'll get you something else." I didn't know which was worse, the pain from vomiting or the physical pain I was suffering from. Both felt as bad as the other.

About an hour later my replacement meal arrived and was much easier on my stomach - thank goodness! Exhausted and sore, I went to sleep and slept well. I remained in hospital for four days due to the pain not subsiding as soon as Dr Harry and I would have liked. I was thankful for private health insurance to allow this to happen with ease and without financial worries. Prior to being discharged, Dr Harry visited me and shared images of a big chunk of endometriosis he had removed between my right ovary and pelvis. No wonder I was experiencing so much pain post surgery!

Perhaps this was why my previous IVF cycles hadn't worked? This took me down a rabbit hole of optimism and misguided faith.

Allow me to explain the procedures I had and why. A dilation and curettage (D&C) is a surgical procedure that removes tissue from the uterus. It's used to diagnose and treat uterine conditions, such as heavy bleeding or an incomplete miscarriage.

A hysteroscopy can be used to investigate symptoms or problems such as:
- heavy periods, unusual vaginal bleeding, postmenopausal bleeding,
- pelvic pain
- repeated miscarriages or
- difficulty getting pregnant
- diagnose conditions – such as fibroids and polyps (non-cancerous growths in the womb)

In my case it was scheduled to investigate the causes of repeated miscarriages and difficulty in falling pregnant. A laparoscopy can be used to diagnose conditions such as appendicitis, pelvic inflammatory disease, endometriosis and some cancers, such as liver cancer and ovarian cancer. In my case, it was to determine if endometriosis was a contributing factor in my failed IVF cycles. And it was.

I was a little surprised at being told endometriosis had been found. I believed that I had never had symptoms that would indicate I was suffering from endometriosis.

A 2020 study (IVF Success Rates) which analysed 36,925 IVF cycles found that fresh eggs have better success rates than frozen eggs: fresh eggs had a 47.7% live birth rate, versus 39.6% for frozen eggs.

When it comes to embryos, fresh embryos have comparable success rates to frozen embryos. However, these statistics don't take several factors into consideration, such as:

- The age of a woman when her eggs were collected, which is one of the most important factors in determining success
- The quality of the eggs and sperm used within treatment
- Age of woman when undertaking a full IVF cycle

You have read in earlier sections of this book that I also underwent acupuncture and took several supplements alongside each of my IVF cycles. Again, this was purely my choice, and I should also mention I saw a naturopath and fertility nutritionist as well.

Role of psychology and energy healing

Adding further to the intricate web that is IVF, at the beginning of 2021, I began seeing a psychologist who specialised in Core Energetics. The reason I did so was after watching the Goop Wellness Series on YouTube (the Gwyneth Paltrow Goop I am talking about here). If you haven't watched her series it truly is fascinating to watch and consider the variety of ways we can explore to better understand our bodies, mind, and self. For me, the Core Energetics segment piqued my curiosity and after researching whether any Psychologists specialised in the field close to me, I discovered an amazing lady I would see for the next two years. She later referred me to my naturopath who also turned out to be an amazing and kind human.

According to the Energetics Institute (Energetics Institute - Psychotherapy and Counselling), Core Energetics is *"a body-mind therapy that addresses how beliefs, feelings and inner life are sustained and reinforced in the body. In childhood, repeated patterns of feelings create specific patterns of muscular tension and weakness in the physical body which relate to trapped emotional memory. These habitual patterns become largely unconscious as we adopt them and then use them later in life to meet our needs. Core Energetics therapy involves the unblocking and releasing of emotion in order to self-heal both physical and mental conditions. This therapy process focuses on unifying and connecting the body, emotions, mind, will/intent, and spiritual self into a unified whole that expresses your complete reality."*

The fascination with core energetics for me was what could be revealed by the body in regards to childhood, trauma and stored wounding. This was later reinforced during my sessions with my psychologist Alana. I think it was only our second session she did a body reading on me. I was truly amazed at what she told me, just by me standing in a sports bra and leggings (she needed to see my mid-region for an accurate reading).

Here's some of what she told me at the reading session.

★ I had a strong male influence in my life up until the age of approximately 8 or 9 nine years of age - this was correct! My dad and maternal grandfather were my absolute loves, and I was beyond devastated when my maternal grandfather passed away. My psychologist said she could tell this due to my large chest which apparently develops from a very young age and with a strong and positive male influence. I never saw that as a reason why I was big-busted.

★ My heart area was closed, possibly from childhood trauma - she was right about my heart being closed off. I was never one to open easily to others and even those closest to me really didn't know the real vulnerable me.

★ My throat area was also closed off - also correct. I was definitely not the person to speak what she was thinking, challenge others, nor say no to anyone or anything.

If you are starting to see a theme here, it does sound a little like a chakra reading, doesn't it? Especially in terms of the heart and throat. This was one of my most favourite sessions with her, one I found so interesting and insightful. When they began to speak and share with me what they could see looking at my body, I noticed my body start to withdraw into itself (figuratively speaking) and I felt exposed, shame, guilt and sadness. It was a bit like having my heart ripped wide open for all to see and all I wanted to do was run away and hide from it all and everyone. I remember we chatted a little after the reading, not for long though. It was quite an intense session for me.

Reading through my journal entries of that time provides some great insights. They reflected a deep awareness of some core aspects of my emotional and physical health, as well as the challenges I've faced in trying to navigate them. The recurring themes of disturbed sleep, nutrition, relationships, and emotional maturity highlight some complex and intertwined issues, as well as a strong sense of introspection and a desire for growth.

"Ongoing disturbed sleep is a major contributor to my emotional state (good or otherwise). No matter how much or how little sleep I get each day and night it doesn't seem to make any difference. I'm tired all the time and feel frustrated that nothing I do works to ease the fatigue. Is this how my life is going to be? If so, I want out of it. How can I be a mum, partner, friend if I am too tired to do

anything? This is bs, surely no one else lives this way. What do I need to do to change things"

I had recognised the significant impact sleep had on how I felt day-to-day. Sleep affected my mood in both positive and negative ways, which was a crucial insight when considering my emotional health. Sleep plays such a crucial role in regulating my emotional well-being, and it's clear that when I'm not sleeping well, it affects my mood and mental clarity. I wondered if it might be worth exploring some sleep hygiene techniques or habits that could help improve my sleep—starting with small adjustments, like setting a consistent bedtime of 9pm and limiting screen time one hour before bed. Both made a big difference in sleep duration and quality.

"My food choices seem to greatly impact my body (positively and negatively) and affect my mood. Eating gluten, primarily wheat, and dairy seems to bloat me, even if I only eat small quantities. I'm also snapping at people for no reason. What is wrong with me! And now my body is rejecting my favourite foods. What the heck am I going to eat that tastes any good now? Bloody hell, it's bad enough I am not sleeping, now I need to restrict what I am eating too. What else do I need to do to have my baby? I bet no one else has had to do this! Why am I being punished?"

I ever so slowly began to notice the strong link between what I ate and how I felt, both physically and emotionally. The awareness of how my body responded to food revealed to me the depth of my understanding of the connection between physical health and mental well-being.

"I solemnly promise to explore my feelings on a deeper level. I will sit with them no matter how uncomfortable it feels".

I must have literally written this at least ten times over a month-long stretch. Followed by, *"Today was not good, I felt teary, anxious and scared. To make myself feel better I bought a bacon and egg roll, the bloating it caused after eating it certainly distracted me the rest of the day. I really hate feeling like this. Like what is wrong with me?"*

The reality of my emotional explorations could not have been more opposite. I remained on the surface, acknowledging their existence and at very rare moments in time, actually feeling them. Not wanting to explore their depths - for fear of what might be unearthed and that it would unravel me in the discovery process. Yes that all sounds a bit dramatic, but this was a real fear of mine.

I was struggling in a powerful internal conflict: the desire to understand my emotions more fully, yet an ever-present fear that doing so could open up something difficult I wouldn't want to face. There was an understandable hesitation to dive deeper, but acknowledging that fear was an important part of the process.

"I know that I need to build a workable and flexible balance between rest and work, but how do I do that? Like what does that even look like? I see so many people on social media promote how they do it as though it's so easy, but it really isn't. Or am I making life hard for myself? I never seem to get the balance just right, is there even a right way? Gosh this is hard! Like it's not like I don't want to feel more ease, calm and effortless simplicity. But with so much to do in and out of work, what do I have to give up? Why can't

I have it all and feel peaceful at the same time. Is that too much to ask? I always thought my ability to multitask was a strength, when instead it is a stressor for me. It has left me feeling tired - physically mentally and emotionally. I'm eating so much processed or junk food because it's quick and easy, not healthy. My body feels so blah, bloated and heavy. My skin looks dull and tired. Actually I look haggard and I'm not that old."

I was struggling to find the right balance between rest and work. I'd been aware of it for a while, but despite my efforts, I hadn't been able to find that sweet spot that worked for me. The acknowledgment of this ongoing challenge showed my determination to eventually get it right.

"Why do I struggle so much around others? Why do I feel scared to speak up and say what I really want to say? I know why, I don't want an argument, someone to yell at me or worse still walk away. I deeply long for a connection with those closest to me, and at the same time am scared to express my vulnerability. What if they judge me, criticise or abandon me? What would I do then? I'm so good at pretending to not feel and just get on with things. I know that repels people or at the very least pushes them away, which I just hate. It makes me feel sad and reaching for chocolate chips isn't giving me the support and distraction it once did - what is going on with that?"

I had a profound desire for deeper relationships, but was also navigating a fear of being vulnerable with others, fearing rejection or judgment. This tension between wanting connection and fearing the vulnerability it required was something I hope you can relate to. It truly felt all consuming, overwhelming, saddening and lonely at times. Something I wouldn't wish on anyone ever.

That was just the tip of the iceberg and the main themes of my psychology sessions, no wonder I left most of them feeling fatigued and drained. I should add though, in the end it was totally worth it for me, the money spent, time travelling across Sydney and the investment in knowing myself was the best gift I have ever given and received.

Our sessions continued for two years and they were an incredible help to release the pain and fear associated with my miscarriage, amongst a few other issues. Using a foam roller to hit a large foam block while reciting "I hate you", "It's not ok" or "No" was liberating to say the least. The vibration felt in my throat alongside the physical release of my anger, rage and hurt was intense. Imagine a burning ember working its way up your chest, travelling up and along your shoulder before burning down your arms. That's exactly what it felt like. I could literally feel the energy moving through my body, it was so powerful. Each session was emotionally exhausting from the tears shed, physical hitting of an object and laying on the floor and having a good old fashioned toddler tantrum. Yes they do work. Laying on a mat stamping my feet and banging my clenched fists on the floor is surprisingly therapeutic. Again, as I engaged in the physical activity and voiced loudly "no" a tingling enveloped me pulsing through every inch of my body until it reached my feet and I could feel the tingling no more.

My miscarriage was greatly triggering for me because I was

scared not only that it might happen again, but also what if I wasn't strong enough to feel the depth of emotions I was so desperately trying to hold onto and avoid letting out? I didn't trust myself that I would be ok if I released the pent-up emotions. I literally felt terrified. They quickly triggered my fear response.

I remember one particular treatment where I was laying on a yoga mat in their treatment room, a blanket covering me from the waist down (for warmth). Alana, my Core Energetics Therapist, sat right beside me, speaking in a soft, hushed tone asking me to describe the miscarriage and feel it in my body, particularly in my heart. Straight away I felt a sudden and strong rise of heat to my chest. It tightened and the tears began to flow. Think of a waterfall and how the water gushes and cascading down, that's how my tears were and felt. A full body sobbing, I was overcome with emotion and wondered if the tears would ever stop, let alone the intensity of them. They asked me to hold myself in that moment and trust I was going to be ok. That triggered further and deeper sobbing that at the time I felt may never stop. They asked me why I was sobbing, and through the tears and short sharp breaths I muttered, "I don't trust I am going to be ok."

And there it was, my fear in its naked glory, fully exposed to be trampled on, healed or loved. That's how it felt anyway. I didn't believe I was going to be ok.

Now I am not sure about you, but feeling so exposed and vulnerable is not one of my favourite pastimes. In fact it is the main thing I would avoid more than anything. *What if people judged me, criticised me, abandoned me?* I felt so stupid for crying over losing a 7-week-old foetus, others had probably suffered greater than me. What made it worse was a comment from a loved one at the time of my miscarriage:

"I know you might not want to hear this, but maybe it was for the best."

What if it was for the best? What if I wasn't meant to be a mum and wouldn't be good enough anyway and that's why I miscarried.

All terrible thoughts!

They then asked if they could place a hand on my arm, before they actually did so. I remember the exact moment they touched my arm and I felt relief, similar to the feeling of when you first step into a warm shower and the comfort from the water running down my body. I was surprised at the impact of a simple touch. They believed in me, perhaps I could believe in me too. Soon after I felt that huge weight lifted from my body, not realising until then just how heavy a weight those feelings were. Feeling exhausted, lighter, and a sense of pride, I did get through it and perhaps could do so again.

I found our sessions incredibly helpful, relieving and insightful as to what I did and why as I was disconnected from myself and operating quite robotically at that point, albeit I didn't even realise it.

Some sessions were just me talking, venting or crying with her helping me to unpack the root issue and emotion to heal. Others were physical in nature, designed to release pent up emotions particularly anger, hurt and frustration. There is nothing quite like hitting a foam pad while visualising your target on it. If you have never done so, the surge of energy that pulses through your body is like no other. For me my anger and frustration always sat in my stomach and I could literally feel it rising through my body, up my chest, along my arms and through the foam bat I was using as the vehicle to expel it from my body.

Other times I was laying on a yoga mat, stamping my feet and hands in what I can only describe as a toddler tantrum while yelling out statements again to expel the negative energy within my body. Now I know this possibly may seem counterintuitive but it actually works. I can't begin to tell you the amount of times I finished a session feeling lighter, tired and more and more positive about myself, my life and the future. Over time we also discussed my IVF cycles and they introduced me to understanding that birthing is the most profound initiation to spirituality a woman can have.

At the start of 2023 I moved to a new job and was no longer able to attend my sessions with as much ease as before. I felt strong in myself emotionally and wondered whether I was now in a position where I could counsel myself using the techniques they had given me. I took a punt on myself and decided to give it a shot.

Role of naturopathy

Alongside my psychologist sessions, I also saw an amazing naturopath who opened my eyes to the benefits of eliminating gluten and dairy from my diet, in order to reduce any likely internal inflammation that may create an issue with my embryos sticking. This was not something I had ever considered up until that point and was willing to try anything to be honest. I so deeply longed for my baby to be in my arms. Literally tell me what I need to do and I'll do it, whatever it takes, whatever it costs. Am I alone in this mindset? Yes I was grasping at straws in the hope they would deliver me my deepest desire.

For a little context, I was never a big gluten and dairy eater so making the decision to go gluten and dairy free wouldn't be a big change for me on a day-to-day basis. So I swapped the bread I ate and the milk I drank. What I did notice within the first month of choosing to eat dairy and gluten free though, was how much more energy I had. My skin looked and felt clearer, my hair breakage reduced and I felt physically lighter. Who knew a simple dietary tweak could have such a large impact?

At the naturopath's suggestion, I expanded my range of supplements to support egg quality and quantity, reduce inflammation, improve gut health, reduce stress and aid implantation. It couldn't hurt right? We continued for a few sessions, assessing any side effects (so dosage could be adjusted if needed). What I learnt from her was the importance of considering my nutrition, not just my medication protocol, and that natural medicine can be better than pharmaceuticals. I thought so anyway.

To this day I am still predominantly gluten and dairy free. Yes I do indulge in the odd hot chip and piece of cheese, experiencing little side effects. I figure life's there to enjoy so why not indulge in moderation. What I do know is that if I indulge too much or too frequently in either gluten or dairy, my body doesn't like it and she's not afraid to tell me either. Now I'm not suggesting if you are going down the IVF path or are trying to conceive to do as I chose to and eliminate gluten and dairy from your diet. Merely I am sharing my thoughts, choices and outcomes with you.

On her advice and following my own research, I expanded my supplement routine to include immune and gut health support, egg quality support and calcium with Vitamin D. I wanted to give my desire to become a mum my best shot and so supplements became a strong part of my repertoire. After a couple of sessions with my naturopath, I made the decision to cease travelling to see her. We exchanged a few emails, and I felt well prepared and informed to move on with my next cycle. That and the travel began to take up a huge part of my time, which I noticed tired me both mentally and physically, which is most definitely not what you need when trying to conceive, naturally or via IVF. I have no regrets about going to see her, as found she became a source of support, guidance, and kindness that I am forever grateful for.

Around the same time I found a fertility nutritionist who underwent IVF to have her gorgeous babies and shared an abundance of advice on IVF prep, egg quality support, nutrition, embryo implantation support online. I started following her on social media, soon realising she would be a prominent feature in my future cycles, in a positive way. She offered a twelve-week program featuring how to prepare for conception, right through to postpartum nutrition. I joined her program, building my knowledge of evidence-based nutrition to feel better on my fertility journey. I made further tweaks to my food choices, introducing smoothies, tofu, and a variety of herbs and spices to my meal prep. Finding them all quite tasty and easy to prepare, they soon became a regular feature in my menu planning and grocery shop. Similar to my experience with the naturopath, these tweaks saw me feel lighter, clear headed, providing me a better quality sleep, and improving my skin tone. Excited to begin my next cycle, I religiously followed the example meal plan and took my supplements.

I discovered Maria through an Optimising Your Fertility webinar she was running and right from the start I found her insightful, practical and very knowledgeable. Tailoring meal plans for preparing for IVF, egg collection and embryo transfer, followed by the first trimester - awesome!

She was extremely kind and generous with her time and knowledge. We had a number of one on one sessions together where I further fine-tuned my food choices and supplements routine. She guided me on the best course of action following the multitude of blood tests I had and I felt in the best shape and preparedness for my upcoming cycle.

Role of acupuncture

The other support I had during my cycles was acupuncture. I had read early on how acupuncture could assist to reduce stress levels and fatigue prior to, during and after an IVF cycle (inclusive of egg collection and embryo transfer). For four cycles I used acupuncture, generally once a week, then just before and right after my embryo transfers. I found each session to be relatively painless, and quite relaxing, a time for me to just lay and be with myself. Focus on deep breathing and sit with my thoughts. Over the course of my sessions I noticed my pulse strengthened which I later realised is also important for a successful cycle. In terms of cost, my private health insurance covered seventy five percent so my out of pocket was manageable for me. The ladies at the clinic were all lovely and very accommodating with last minute changes to procedures. As someone who detests needles I find it quite ironic that not only did I choose to do multiple IVF cycles, plus acupuncture as well. Glutton for punishment or brave for conquering a lifelong fear.

Five cycles down and still not a mum, with so many thoughts swirling around my mind, what to do, where to turn, the timing of it all. I just wanted to fall into a heap and cry.

> *Do I try for another fertility specialist? If so, who?*
> *Do I push for different medication protocols?*
> *Do I consider donor eggs?*
> *Do I look into adoption instead?*
> *Do I try to fall naturally? Is that even possible?*
> *Do I push for further testing (e.g. Emma, Alice, ERA)?*
> *Is any of the above even feasible?*

After a heated phone call with my fertility specialist, I felt deflated, defeated and not heard. I requested a call from Dr Lee.

Dr Lee: "How can I help you today Dianne?"

Me: "Thanks Dr Lee, I appreciate you taking the time to speak with me. We have done a couple of cycles now and I believe with each one the embryo has implanted and as soon as I cease taking medication my pregnancy symptoms disappear within a couple of days."

Dr Lee: " Yes, and as I have explained to you before, the odds of success at your age are less than five per cent using your own eggs."

Me: "Yes I understand that, and am wondering if we can test my progesterone levels prior to my next cycle to determine if they warrant an increase to aid in implantation and pregnancy?"

Dr Lee: "As I have told you before, your age affects the number and quality of your eggs. The medication protocol we have been using with you is the best way if you continue to use your own eggs. Again, as I have told you, donor eggs will give you a greater chance of success."

Me: "I understand all of that but can't we at least do a blood test to check? It's not costly nor invasive and who knows it may make the difference?"

Dr Lee: "Should you wish to do another cycle, I will not be looking to change medication protocols."

Me: "Ok, thank you".

I hung up, feeling incredibly frustrated and unheard. I wonder at times whether even the fertility specialists themselves have become immune to the emotional roller coaster of IVF and what it means to us, their clients, who dream of parenthood and need some help to get there. Yes, we are fragile and sometimes that might be frustrating for the specialist, but I urge them to stop and just listen. Listen to what your patient is asking of or telling you. It is coming from their heart which is hurting, confused, frustrated or a mix of all the above. Be patient, and above all please be kind. It was at that moment that I researched contact details for another fertility specialist whose expertise in older mums and donor conception was world-renowned.

Supporting mental health through IVF

Following my anxiety and depression diagnosis back in 2016 I was prescribed medication, which was its own gauntlet of trials and testing to see which one worked for me, the dosage that didn't leave me feeling like a zombie or worse nauseous. I finally landed on Zoloft which I had few side effects from taking, albeit I was on a small dose, enough to keep me balanced without feeling groggy - perfect! Following my numerous cycles I discovered it would be in my best interests (also in consultation with my GP and psychologist) to increase my dose slightly to aid me riding the emotional waves of IVF while at the same time working to build my emotional resilience and courage. I did find that I was snapping less at people and myself after increasing my dosage while at the same time feeling guilty that I couldn't better manage my emotions. Oh the joys of life and self critiquing.

I was doing everything physically I could do to become a mum, perhaps at times a little too much. I was holding onto blind faith and repeating the same process over and over again. I was beginning to take myself down another path of invasive and costly testing to solve my problem, without even knowing for sure it was something I in fact even needed. My repetitive

self-diagnosed Google process looked like:
- Eliminating all junk and processed foods (minimise internal inflammation, increase my egg quality and quantity, and support healthy embryo implantation). Numerous websites referenced this and surely they were right? It wasn't just one article, it was literally hundreds
- Attending weekly acupuncture sessions - these were meant to strengthen my pulse and unblock stagnant blood flow, potentially inhibiting my fertility. I self diagnosed this, based solely on Dr Google telling me that was the cause of my infertility. I should add I completely ignored my age in my online research. That surely couldn't be the cause (and something I couldn't change), I focused on the causes I could change: my diet, exercise, supplement intake etc.
- Increasing intake of avocados (a good source of folate, healthy fats and vitamin E to increase my chance of a live birth after embryo implantation. More self diagnosis)
- Maintaining the same medication protocols each cycle - who was I to challenge a doctor! I believed he knew what he was doing and had done it many times before with success so maybe it's a numbers game and the more times I give it a go, the better chances of my success? Deep down I desperately wanted to try infusions, progesterone and testing to see why my body wasn't falling pregnant. I felt she was the problem and if I could just do or take something to fix it then we'd be on the right path
- Listening to fertility meditations before bed each night - I strongly believed that by playing these every day and sometimes twice daily it would implant something

in my head and body that I am pregnant - a little like subliminal messaging
- At home fertility yoga sessions three to four times a week - I was convinced these along with my meditation sessions would guarantee success! They were both targeting fertility so how could they not work. And when I say they were targeting fertility, the title of the yoga and meditations had the word fertility in them.

That was what hooked me in, it's like everything I read I was scanning for the word fertility and when I saw it, I latched onto it tightly, afraid to let go. To me that meant they were specifically designed to aid success with no other thought on my part as to whether that was reality or not. At the same time I felt I was going through the motions with no real connection to my body. It was almost like I was trying to force my body to do what I was desperately willing it to do, whether it wanted to or even could do. That I gave no consideration for whatsoever.

Equally I wasn't focusing at all on my emotional or mental state which are also the driving force to an aligned body, mind and soul connection. Searching for answers like if I could just do X then Y will happen. Life doesn't work like that, well it didn't for me anyway and it seems to be a common theme when looking back at my journal entries for all five cycles. Now this has been a recurrent theme throughout my life. Take my weight loss when I lost 23 kilos in six months, all through the physical action of dieting, exercise and then looking in the mirror and seeing the same size 14 woman looking back (by then I was a size 8-10). I didn't see the difference in my body. Why? I hadn't even considered my mental state and mindset as part of this journey, let alone redefining it as developing a slim self-image as opposed to a weight-loss journey. These was so much to consider and adjust to.

I realised that my body was telling me that it needed to rest and recharge. I was crying at the drop of a hat, snapping at anyone and everyone, easily frustrated by the simplest of tasks, waking multiple times a night and eating fast food like it was going out of fashion. I kept telling myself to just keep going, the business shutdown period wasn't that far away (six weeks) and I had already survived most of the year. One day while at work and compiling some meeting papers my Adobe PDF editor wasn't working, and I needed it to compile some business papers for an upcoming meeting. On this particular day that was the straw that broke the camel's back. I broke down in tears and said to my colleague, "I can't do this anymore."

She turned to me and said, "No you can't and you shouldn't."

I looked at her with shock and intrigue, she was agreeing with me. Was I worse than I thought? She finalised the business papers for me while I sat in the kitchen and calmed down over a herbal tea. Normally I would reach for coffee, but that day something was telling me caffeine wouldn't help. I sat near the window where I could see the people walking on the footpath below. The change in scenery was a welcome distraction from emotional overwhelm. I returned back to my desk.

"I'm going to speak to our boss about reducing my work days between now and the end of the year," I said.

"I think that is a great idea for you," my colleague said.

"I'll make some time to talk with her tomorrow and give

myself today to gather my thoughts. I am feeling quite emotional and not ready to ask yet."

This self-discovery became the catalyst for talking with my boss about working four days instead of five days a week for the remainder of the year (five weeks in total).

The next day I saw my boss walk past and asked if we could chat briefly. Thankfully she agreed.

"I was wondering if it would be possible for me to reduce my work days from five days to four or even three if that is possible? I am struggling with a lot outside of work at the moment and I feel I am not at my best here and would love the opportunity to take some time to rest, heal, recharge and relax," I explained.

"I can see you haven't been yourself of late and I have been worried about you. I think reducing your days to four days a week is a good idea and we can definitely manage that. In terms of three days a week, can we start with four and then see how we can redistribute workload to support you if you like?"

I was relieved.

"Oh my god, thank you so much for listening to me. I really appreciate it, and yes I am happy to work with you on how this can best work for both of us."

Between my colleague and I we reconfigured our work and how we could check in each week with how things were tracking (both inside and outside of work).

Interestingly I found I was able to complete more work, possibly due to the guilt of my colleague remaining working five days, and also I feel I saw it as a reward to myself if I worked hard then I deserved the extra time I was taking off work.

Funny how our minds work. It wasn't a matter of my deserving anything. I needed it, plain and simple. I had pushed myself too far. I saw the early signs of a potential breakdown and I did not want to go back there ever. I was doing what I needed to do for myself. To stop, just stop.

I had put my body through so much already, it wasn't a lot to ask was it? I should add that it wasn't just the stress of IVF affecting me, my job itself was quite a chaotic and at times extremely demanding one with multiple time pressures and external considerations needing to be woven into document preparation and in the manner in which meetings were held. A slower pace to end 2021 was much needed, and thankfully, they accommodated. I had pushed my body to its limit, not recognising the signs, telling myself it was just a busy time for me and it would pass.

CHAPTER 4

Letting go and rediscovering my path

"If you want to fly, you have to give up what weighs you down"

– UNKNOWN

During 2021, I did toy around with the idea of finding someone, a partner and a few girlfriends suggested I consider casual dating. The thought process at the time was I might fall pregnant that way and at least I would know the dad, even if he chose not to be involved in my child's life. It would also save an incredible amount of money I could use elsewhere in my life. I understood the logic behind this and did briefly consider exploring that path. But that just wasn't me, I was never the sort of girl who wanted a casual fling with anyone, I wanted a relationship. It was time for me to admit that to myself and start living my truth. For me the only positive I found in that scenario was my child would know who their dad was, what I then spent time deeply reflecting on was would this be the way for me to have a child? Could I actually do this?

It could be, yes, but ultimately no I couldn't. Actually, maybe not that I couldn't but I didn't see that as the right option for me. I wasn't the sort of person to just have sex with someone to have a baby, no matter how much I wanted to make that ok in my head. It just wasn't me. I had also realised that even if I went down that path, my eggs were part of the issue and no casual fling would solve that. Five cycles using my own eggs, each time my fertility specialist telling me perhaps I should consider donor eggs due to my age and lack of success with IVF. Doing my own research on the rates of success for older mums conceiving using their own eggs wasn't entirely impossible but the likelihood was pretty slim. My doctor once told me "What is more important to you - becoming a mum or using your own eggs? That's what you need to consider."

At the end of the day I wanted to be a mum, and that decision, knowledge and awareness was ultimately what led me down the donor conception path. It was more important for me to become a mum than to use my eggs. That desire, longing, drive - whatever you want to call it, was more powerful.

Considering a donor path

I purchased a beautiful IVF Journal by the company 'Write to Me' at the very start of my IVF journey to capture my thoughts, consultation notes, medications and so on. I found it incredibly helpful to have everything in one place and later look back on and reflect on just how far I have come and how my thoughts and actions have evolved over time. Recurring themes for self-care included choosing nourishing foods, resting, daily movement and connecting with my intuition to guide me each day.

So here I was five cycles down, no baby and feeling incredibly frustrated, lost and just sad. After three years of trying, I was beginning to wonder whether it was ever going to happen, and if not, what was I going to do. I never for once believed it would be this hard, long or costly. I knew I was blessed to be living in a country with a supportive public healthcare system complemented with a private health care system. My out of pocket costs were a lot less than I know many others had to pay - one of the benefits for being classed as 'geriatric' and 'socially infertile' as someone trying to get pregnant over 40. It was the only benefit to be really honest. My eggs were there in numbers, just not in quality and it began to dawn on me quickly there wasn't a lot I could do about it. Yes I could

LETTING GO AND REDISCOVERING MY PATH

improve my nutrition to support egg quality, complemented by a variety of supplements, acupuncture and naturopathy. At the end of the day, I was well into my 40s and the odds were against me (albeit not impossible) to conceive using my own eggs. *Sure it may happen, but how long was I willing to continue cycle after cycle until it did? And most importantly what would the cost emotionally and mentally be for me in doing so? Would it be worth it in the end, and would it result in my precious baby? Would it result in me ending up not being a mum at all?*

That was not a thought or feeling that sat well with me, so to some degree life forced me to reconsider my path. It was at this point I started to consider fostering, adoption, surrogacy and donor conception. Now when I say I started to consider it, admittedly, it was light hearted at first as I still believed that I could have a child of my own using my eggs. At that time I wasn't ready to let that belief go. On the surface, I thought to myself:

"It doesn't really matter, did it? As long as I have my beloved baby does it matter how that happens?"

It did matter though. More than I thought. The deeper I probed into that question, the more I felt it sting my heart. The thought of using donor eggs made me feel incredible guilt towards my future baby. I felt like somehow I had let him or her down by doing so. *What would they think of me, themselves and their place in life?*

Not easy questions to wrap your head around, let alone answer easily and quickly. I also felt guilt and fear around how I may be judged by others, including those close to me for deciding to explore the donor path. As I mentioned earlier IVF remains a topic that isn't openly discussed let alone the donor path, which seems to have a greater stigma attached to it - hence creating a lot of fear within me.

Now I am not knocking anyone who may or may not have gone through a similar journey to me, everyone is entitled to their opinion. From my own experience in life and online, there are some misconceptions, misinformation and hurtful judgements out there which I believe have no place in this discussion. Again, these are my thoughts and mine alone; you are free to agree or disagree, that's the beauty of life.

So where did I start, you may wonder? It really was that question - *"Dianne, what's more important to you, being a mum or having a baby using your own eggs?"*

The question really stuck with me and swirled around in my brain for many months while I worked through letting go of how I thought it would all happen and be prepared to take an alternate route on my road of motherhood. Why couldn't I have both? Now I would love to say it all happened super-fast and I was back doing another cycle again. It didn't quite work that.

There was a lot of mental toing and froing, initially on a practical level (i.e. how would it all work, timing of all the parts, cost, and risks). Not having landed on a decision either way, I was juggling this mental load alone. In part I wasn't sure what I wanted to do, and also I didn't want to face any judgement from anyone while working through my thoughts and feelings, particularly until I had landed on what was going to be best for me. Fear played a very big part in this.

LETTING GO AND REDISCOVERING MY PATH

I began to research the intricate web of donor conception, all the while knowing that I could choose to remain within the same fertility clinic, albeit working with another specialist. What I did know at that stage was that my current specialist was not the best one for me. I needed someone who would listen to my thoughts and questions, and be open to exploring different medication protocols, not just lumping me in the 'too old' basket and leaving it at that. Perhaps someone who was more specialised in donor conception. I remembered reading that my fertility clinic did have a couple of options for specialists in this area.

I joined a couple of donor Facebook groups to start understanding the process.

Would I seek my own donor or stay with a fertility clinic? There seemed to be pros and cons to both avenues. Should I consider going overseas? It seemed that Greece and South Africa had amazing results using donor eggs compared to the US and here in Australia. There was so much to consider.

Here's just a sample of the thoughts that consumed me at this time:

Where would I even go to source the eggs?

How would I even get them?

How long would it take, cost?

What if I can't find suitable ones?

How would I then source the donor sperm, and how long would that take?

Would I need to undergo genetic testing again? I know from last time, that took quite a while to complete.

What if I am not a suitable candidate for donor conception?

What if this doesn't work, then what?

Do I consider bypassing donor eggs and going straight for donor embryos?

How do I even begin to tell people about me undergoing donor conception?

What would they think of and say about me and my future baby?

Would we be disowned? If so, how on earth would I manage?

What if my future baby wasn't accepted into the family and my trusted circle of friends?

Is it even fair that I explore doing this? What would the effect of my decision be on my future baby? Would they hate me for doing this?

What if my body fails me again?

What if I can't find a specialist who will listen to me?

How long am I prepared to keep trying for a baby?

I can now see how these thoughts began to consume me. It was mentally, emotionally and physically draining. I felt that time was not on my side and perhaps I needed to hurry and make a decision, or I would miss out. I should disclose that none of this rush came from the fertility clinic, it was solely coming from me - all driven by fear that I may miss out, which felt heartbreaking to me.

I chose to seek other professional opinions, knowing for sure I would not be continuing with my current specialist. I spoke with a lovely lady based in the city, still with the same fertility clinic. I found her demeanour and our interaction so much more positive, inspiring and open-minded. Where I had hoped it was merely implantation issues, it seemed when reviewing my cycle history in full (which my previous doctor never did nor offered me), it was more likely that my embryos were defective. Funnily enough this meant I was a good candidate for donor eggs as implantation did not appear to be an issue for my body (Yay – something good at least!)

She advised me to amend my medication protocol in order to assist implantation and I felt instant anger towards my previous doctor who hadn't even considered, let alone offered me this. His thought was I was too old so I should go straight to donor eggs. What I did find disappointing was the overseas donor bank they used for eggs and sperm did not have the best results for success and she referred me to another doctor/clinic who I would later use and have my precious Eva. I am deeply grateful to her for her honesty and for recommending that I use another clinic. She could have taken me on, and her suggestion to go elsewhere was refreshing and daunting.

My journal entry for that day read:

"My darling baby, I want you more than anything and hope you will always know that. Mummy is trying her best to bring you earthside. My heart aches for you and I just want to hold you in my arms."

Not long after, I began comfort eating to mask the sadness, emptiness, disappointment and frustration I felt. Eating my emotions seemed to be the easiest solution. A good distraction if you like. It was so much better than actually feeling them. That was just too much to bear.

I knew that wasn't the best way to treat my body, which had done so much for me but I didn't care. I just didn't want to feel bad and choosing corn chips, chocolate and fried food was deliciously satisfying. I hate to admit that later that night I was regretting my choice, my body felt heavy, bloated, uncomfortable and slightly painful - damn gluten!

Remaining with my feelings, especially the really difficult ones was hard, bloody hard and that's ok. The important thing was to acknowledge and feel them, in their entirety. Our feelings are present to teach us all a lesson and will often leave once the lesson is learnt.

I regularly tracked my progesterone levels during each of my cycles as well as any physical symptoms. This did prove helpful on one hand, and a little consuming and overwhelming on the other. I was fixated on the numbers, again as a means of control, thinking I had control that is. I didn't.

My mind was constantly ticking over about taking more time for me to rest, allowing things to happen, releasing the stress of work and what I expected to happen. Thoughts swirling around with nowhere to land, like a buzzing bee unable to find any nectar to refresh and rejuvenate it. That was me. Numerous Google searches on pregnancy symptoms, why I wasn't falling pregnant, and what I could eat to guarantee success were no help at all. If anything, they added to the swirling thoughts consuming me. No wonder I was so stressed and anxious.

I had been ruminating on this for quite some time, trying to process my thoughts and feelings about IVF, donor conception, timing etc. It was deeply triggering my need and want to control, when in reality there was very little I could control. Mixing this with a colleague falling pregnant (seemingly quite easy) and another beginning her own IVF journey was a little heartbreaking. Don't get me wrong I was stoked for both of them, while at the same time envious and jealous why it wasn't easy for me. Note to self here, you never know what happens behind closed doors so assumptions can often be misleading. The lesson for me at this time was to surrender and trust what will be.

I was truly blessed with the openness of a couple of good friends who shared their own journey to motherhood, the pros and cons. What I found most interesting was how they mentioned how a lot of people commented on how much their children look like them. This was something I hadn't even considered when thinking about donor conception. I began to wonder about my genetic makeup and how that would transfer to my precious bubba. *Would they share the same mannerisms as me, look like me?* I began to toss up whether to access a clinic or advertise for donor eggs. The pros in advertising was I would know the donor and possibly enjoy a relationship with them and their family (including any children they have). This was quite appealing to me, as I was torn whether my child may struggle with their identity and if it would help and support them to know the egg donor and their siblings. Which way would you go? It is not an easy question to answer.

Deciding to go down the donor path

Fast forward a few months and I thought to myself: *Yep, I'm ready.* I felt good about choosing to go down the donor path. *Let's go!* My goodness if only it was that easy.

I told a friend whom I had met through a Facebook business group of my plans to explore the donor conception path after having tried multiple IVF cycles using my own eggs. Funny who life connects you with, as she shared with me that she had conceived her children also via IVF using her own eggs. They were about to start school and I felt a strong sense of hope and optimism pulse through my body. If she could do it, surely I could too! She had developed an interest in tapping during her journey to and post motherhood and was passionate about introducing the benefits to other women, particularly those undertaking IVF.

EFT

Everyday Health online group defines tapping (known as Emotional Freedom Technique - EFT) as a mind-body therapy that draws on the traditional Chinese medicine (TCM) practice of acupuncture, and it is used today as a self-help approach in modern psychology. It involves tapping key acupressure points (acupoints) on the hands, face, and body with your fingertips while focusing on uncomfortable feelings or concerns, and using positive affirmations to neutralise those feelings. (Source: Everyday Health n.d.) Sounds easy and a bit woo woo doesn't it? Like how can tapping my face or body shift what I am feeling?

Sceptical at first whether simply tapping certain parts of my face would do anything at all, I was more than pleasantly surprised at my results. After a couple of sessions I felt emotionally lighter, and physically tired from releasing the

LETTING GO AND REDISCOVERING MY PATH

deep feelings I didn't know were there. During our first session she explained to me that we would be tapping the same spot seven times before moving onto the next one and we would be using both a set up phrase and a reminder phrase. The set-up (SU) phrase was the first thing we said when tapping on the side of the hand and was repeated three times before moving on to the other points. One set-up (SU) I used during donor IVF was:

SU1: Even though I never expected I would need IVF to have a baby, I thought I would meet a man, fall in love and have babies the traditional way, I deeply and completely love and accept myself.

SU2: Even though I am sad that I left it too late to have a biological child using my eggs, and people close to me think I am too old to have a baby, and it's been a difficult and lonely journey, I want to love and accept myself with compassion.

SU3: Even though I am angry that medical professionals who have not listened to me on my journey to have a baby, and maybe that was because I didn't advocate well for myself, I want to love and accept myself with compassion.

Followed by reminder phrases, where were statements that I believed to be true about myself and my situation. Following the above set-up phrases I continued with:

This fertility journey has been overwhelming. At times, I have felt isolated and very lonely. I never thought I would be doing this by myself, or that those close to me would not understand or support me. I never knew how difficult it would be. I never knew how much it would hurt, physically, financially and emotionally. It has been so damn hard.

Case in point my true feelings about using donor eggs as

we continued through the tapping points I suddenly burst into tears - it did matter and I hadn't fully let go of it yet. Deep, sobbing tears were soon flowing. My chest felt heavy and hurt. My friend gave me the gift of silence to allow my emotions to surface without judgement, critique or discussion. She just allowed me to be with myself and express what I needed to, which in that moment was tears of sorrow, frustration and disappointment in myself.

I have always believed that I would be a mum, using my own eggs, albeit with a partner, but choosing to use donor sperm was no big deal for me - truly. I never considered that it wouldn't work out that way, that my age would play such a significant factor and I would need to make a route adjustment to achieve my desire. And when faced with the reality that I might, it still didn't register as the big deal it actually was! A pattern was repeating – I was going through surface level acknowledgement again, without delving deep into my feelings (I was an expert at this).

Umm no Dianne, it doesn't work that way.

Back to my friend, she was a huge support on my path to donor conception, sharing her own fertility experience, later donating nursery furniture and clothing for my precious Eva. I think because of her experience to conceive I trusted her, and allowed her to probe to unearth deep-seated feelings. I greatly enjoyed our sessions together and am extremely proud of the discoveries I made about myself with her support. She was one of the key people, I believe, who helped me to conceive and subsequently birth a healthy baby girl - for that I am truly grateful!

LETTING GO AND REDISCOVERING MY PATH

So I took a number of months to consider my options and within that my donor options regarding clinic, location, etc. There really is just so much to consider, even more so than IVF which if you have been down that path, you already know how complicated it is. What I soon came to realise was how deeply I longed to be a mum and perhaps was ready to let go of my desire to do so using my own eggs if it meant my dream of motherhood would be fulfilled. It's not like my child wouldn't know how loved they are and how they came into the world. Despite my fears of going down the donor path, one thing I was 100 per cent certain of was that she/he would know their history and have access to their donor details, profiles etc should they wish to. I never wanted to impart my fears onto them, which in hindsight, I think helped me to reach my decision.

Revisiting what my fertility specialist had said to me very early on, what was most important to me was becoming a mum and with time apparently not on my side, following a path different to what I had originally thought maybe wasn't such a bad thing after all. I never thought it was a bad thing ever, at the time or when I actually started the process.

Donor path explained

So here I was ready to embark on the donor path, and double donor path at that. My decision to remain with a fertility clinic throughout the process really came down to timing. I had placed an ad for an egg donor on a reputable Facebook group site. My ad included the qualities I was looking for in my egg donor.

I was looking for someone who had similar features for me in terms of hair and eye colour, was in good health and preferably had children of their own (for me this meant they were fertile and I may have a higher chance of success with their eggs).

It was a bit of an odd experience if I am totally honest. It was almost like a dating profile, where to have any success you need to be very active on the site and posting regular updates about what you are doing in order to remain front of mind to potential donors. If not, you move down the list on the screen. It's quite competitive and in the end I found it extremely exhausting and emotionally draining. Think of a merge between Facebook and a dating profile where you are 'selling' yourself to a donor to choose you and all the while trying to remain relevant for them to want to know more about.

I ended up meeting with my fertility doctor for an initial consultation a day earlier than originally scheduled. Yay! Luck seemed to already be conspiring with me. At the same time I completed my egg donor registration form for the clinic I would be purchasing the eggs from. They were based in the UK and sourced eggs from Europe, shipping them worldwide. It's just crazy to even think about this process and the generosity of women to donate something so precious and personal to another woman they will likely never meet. The company I chose had the highest success rate due to their shipment of the eggs to Australia. As I discovered, many clinics ship their frozen eggs in the cargo hold which may damage the structure of the eggs due to the lower temperature and oxygen levels. My clinic sends the eggs with an actual person to travel as carry on luggage so pressurisation doesn't damage them and they remain stable.

I never even thought this was a thing, but it is. What an amazing job to have!

The egg donor registration form was quite comprehensive and asked me to record what physical characteristics I wanted, including the child's potential wants and needs both in the short and long term. Would having the same hair and eye colour matter to me? This took me a few days to complete as I wanted to be intentional in my choice and not just consider myself, but also my future child. It was a big decision for both of us. I paid my registration fee and that was it, now to just wait until I reached the top of the list. This could be a number of months away I was advised, which wasn't a surprise. This was only a small part of the puzzle as I was also considering at the same time my potential sperm donor and what characteristics I wanted from him. Now, using an egg donor, there were three of us in the picture and it took me some time to figure out how I might be able to blend it all together. If I could, that is. At that time I was feeling positive and believed I could. Blind faith, stubbornness, or perseverance? I do admit I was pinning all of my hopes on this magic egg that would see me become a mum. *Was that even possible, let alone realistic?*

Time ticked along, life carried on and after four months of waiting, anticipating and praying I received an email saying I was now at the top of the egg donor list (YIPPEE!). I already knew it could take up to six months to reach the top of the list, which when I first lodged my application, didn't seem that long away. My goodness though, when you are desperately longing for something so dear to you so much, six months feels like a lifetime. Thankfully for me, the news was earlier than expected, falling on my birthday, what a beautiful gift! It's like it was meant to be, divine timing!

This meant I would soon hear of my choice of available egg donors. I came across numerous success stories of older mums having babies which gave me so much hope it could happen to me too. I began to think of ways I could further improve my nutrition. *Was that even possible? Was it improving or would I be returning to restricting what I ate?* Two very different schools of thought, one healthy, one not so much.

I received three egg donor profiles via email, all of which contained so much more information than I had hoped for. Both baby, child and adult pictures were included - this helped me greatly in deciding, I must say! Looking at the initial three contenders, none were a standout which was a little disappointing. There was nothing wrong with them, they were ok. That was the point, they were just ok. I think I was expecting some sort of connection with one of them, like a hallelujah moment when I saw them and knew they were the one. Is that even realistic to think and want? Was that more pie in the sky type thinking or showing me a deep want of mine from my donor angel? I was faced with a choice: choose one of these and move on or ask for another three profiles. In asking for another three profiles that meant I relinquished my first dibs on them so to speak. In other words if I later wanted one of them, I ran the risk someone else may have chosen them instead. Not that I was ever expecting to be able to hold onto my choices for an indefinite period of time, but I did have a matter of days to make my decision either for one of them or request another three profiles to review.

I remember just how daunting that choice was and combined with a feeling of being pressured to rush or hurry into it. The fertility clinic was amazing and never placed this pressure on me. More so, this was the process, request three profiles and be allotted a few days to decide before proceeding or choosing another three (and relinquishing the first three). I knew I was putting the pressure on myself; I didn't want to miss out. My brain was in overdrive.

What if I get this wrong? What if I still fail? How do I know who is the right choice for me? Gosh how does anyone actually do this; it's not like I'm choosing what to eat for dinner. This is a lifetime decision I am making. I don't know what I am doing. It can't be this hard, stupid.

I decided to sleep on it, knowing all too well I was in a highly emotional space at that time and might not be making the best decision for me and bubs or our future by panicking and rushing into anything. This was a huge deal after all. This amazing, generous and kind woman who I may never meet may enable me to have my deeply longed for child. It was well worth the time, and in reality what harm would it do to see how I felt in the morning. I'd waited this long!

It never ceases to amaze me what a good night's sleep can do for the mind and body. After delighting in a restful sleep I woke refreshed, clear headed and knew exactly what the best decision for me was. I emailed the clinic seeking another three profiles and acknowledged I was relinquishing my exclusive right to the first three. I felt good in my body as I typed out the email and knew in my heart I had done the right thing for me. I am also continually amazed at how when I connect back to myself and breathe deeply, clear decisions make themselves known to me. I feel it in my body, especially my heart and throat chakras. There is no doubt, second guessing myself, instead replaced by certainty and calmness. Do you ever experience this too?

So I waited to receive my next three profiles which came later that same morning. Upon opening the second of the three profiles my heart skipped a beat. I had found her, my donor angel! She had dark, wavy hair just like me and similar facial structure and eyes. Have you ever experienced a sensation when you feel something is right in your body? I don't know about you, for me I felt a warmth through my heart, my shoulders relaxed, my breathing slow and an almost instant sensation of peace. She was here at last, she was the one. Again, deciding not to rush into anything based on pure emotion, I decided to sleep on it and see how I felt in the morning. I awoke the next day with such excitement the decision was easy made. There was no doubt about it, she was the one.

This was a much more emotional process than I gave credit for, and so much more than my previous IVF cycles. I put a lot of pressure on myself to make the 'right' decisions. I felt like the weight of the rest of my life and my future child's life and wellbeing was on my shoulders. It mattered what I ate or didn't, what supplements I took and when, how often I had my acupuncture sessions, how full I allowed my calendar to get each day/ week. My goodness I was exhausted just thinking about it all. I honestly believed that this all mattered in me being successful at becoming a mum via IVF.

Consumed by what I was seeing on social media, reading Dr Google, and talking with friends who had ventured down similar paths. I was frantic, anxious, overwhelmed and experiencing some really uncomfortable gut issues from everything I was doing (or not doing).

Bloated, lower back pain and a never-ending tiredness, my next cycle I was determined to cut myself some slack (or at the very least try to). I would stop doing things just because' and instead ask myself "why am I doing this? Is it something I truly want to do? What do I think I will gain by doing it?" The thoughts that crept in surprised me. I didn't want to do acupuncture anymore; I didn't feel relaxed when I was there. I was too focused on what I needed to do when I got home, or what I needed to organise for work the next day. Kind of defeats the point of balancing my energy and steadying my pulse. Quite the opposite was happening. I noticed my body no longer wanted to do it and when I decided to stop booking anymore sessions I felt relieved having one less thing to do.

Clearly I was doing too much and I needed to listen to my body more about what she truly needed and wanted. Not that I am devaluing acupuncture by any means. For the sessions I did do in the early days, I felt relaxed and enjoyed the time to just breathe and be. Over time it did help to regulate and increase my pulse. Perhaps that period of time served a need that I had at the time, and now I no longer needed it. Not every lasts forever does it?

I realised how much I was pinning my hopes on this magic egg that would give me my baby. That it would give me what my supplements, acupuncture, gluten and dairy free diet hadn't to date. If only it were that easy! You would have thought by now I would know that there were no magic fixes. And yet I was still looking and hoping for one; that's how deep my desire for motherhood was. I would literally do or eat anything that would make me a mum.

But what if I was to change that thinking? What if I decided to do only what felt right? That felt light in my body and a resounding YES! I knew I would face a few mindset obstacles, having thought from a deficit model for so long and expecting external factors to bring me success. *But I could at least try, couldn't I?* I became more aware of how I was thinking about what I was doing, which was the first step in shifting my thoughts patterns, habits and beliefs.

A surprise gift came on my birthday when I reached the top of the sperm donor list (woohoo!), receiving sixteen choices based on my genetic profile (I had sent my genetic test results as part of my sperm donor application). This meant that these sixteen donors posed no concerns with mine, nor the egg donor's, genetics, and so, in theory, resulted in a healthy embryo once the egg was fertilised with the sperm (fingers crossed).

Reading their profiles was awesome, I must say, seeing both baby and adult photos was really helpful. Similar to the egg donor profiles there was an abundance of information on health, education, interests, family history (including health issues if relevant), aspirations for any future offspring (deriving from their donation), and fertility history. Think of it like a dating profile on steroids, and super helpful I must say. For me it certainly made my decision a whole lot easier and also helped reassure me that my future child would appreciate having the information available to them too.

What was I looking for in my sperm donor:
- Dark hair and eyes
- Similar skin tone
- Caring person
- Community and family-minded
- Well educated
- No health conditions
- Lives an active lifestyle
- Non-smoker and non-drinker
- No drug use
- Interest in reading & art

Embodying a similar process as when selecting my egg donor, I narrowed my choices down from sixteen to five, ranked them in order of my initial preference and then slept on it for two days. From the get-go go there was one clear standout, so to make sure this was who I truly wanted, I took a step back and allowed my intuition to guide me rather than my head. My reason for doing so was that I knew at the time my impatience to push ahead would cloud a rational well well-thought-out out decision so I tapped into my heart and gut. I am so glad that I did. Both the egg and sperm donor I chose are exactly who I was meant to find and use, and I couldn't be happier with my choice.

So donor selection was made. It was now time to pay my deposit for the eggs (eight eggs in total was the package I chose). My choice in the donor clinic was because their guarantee was the best around. For the eight eggs I purchased, they guaranteed at least three viable embryos would result, followed by a pregnancy. If not, they would send a replacement eight eggs for another cycle. Feeling flutters in my stomach I paid my deposit, eagerly awaiting the egg shipment date which would be in approximately two to three months' time. *YIPPEE!*

At this point I decided a 30-day cleanse was well and truly in order. I had had both COVID-19 vaccines by this time, experiencing yucky side effects with both doses. Compiled with the array of supplements and IVF meds I had been taking the past few years, my body needed a restart and a good flush out. I know there are a lot of cleanse programs on the market and my body doesn't respond well to fasting, juice cleanses or shakes. So, I designed my own, nothing fancy or special in any way, other than it was clean, wholesome food. No gluten or dairy, limited sugar, and no processed foods - all homemade, good quality and fresh fruit, vegies, protein and legumes. Boy, didn't my body thank me for it. I think back to then as I write and consider embodying more of that now daily. Less junk and low-quality foods, more conscious choices and habit of quality ingredients, minimally processed foods and upping my fruit and veggie intake. Back to basics, really, like how I grew up.

Excited this wasn't taking as long as I first thought. I recall having a dream only a few days earlier that my eggies were being shipped earlier than expected. This particular dream was quite vivid. I could see a plane in the distance and felt excited for its arrival. Unsure why in the beginning but as the plane got closer to the ground the excited tingling through my body grew. During my dream I looked up past the plane and noticed how blue the sky was, how bright the sun was beaming and the warmth I felt on my face looking at it. It was such a glorious feeling! I stood back as I watched the plane land on the empty runway, noticing no one else was around, just me. A side door opened and a set of stairs unfolded from the door. It all happened so quickly.

A flight attendant descended the stairs with a carton of eggs, carrying them ever so carefully and I felt confused. Why was a flight attendant carrying eggs like they were precious cargo? She smiled at me and handed me the egg carton. As she did, the most golden beam of light blessed the egg carton. As she ascended the stairs to return to the plane, she turned to me.

"These are what you have been waiting for. We didn't want you to wait any longer," and she closed the plane door behind her. I looked down at the carton in my hands and felt a rush of energy race through my body. I woke up smiling, then drifted back to sleep.

Exactly one month later, I received my egg shipment date for July 2022. Now it was coming true! Intuition perhaps, or the universe conspiring to work with me? This was also an exciting time, as it meant I could now lock in my chosen sperm donor. To celebrate I bought myself a bunch of flowers; this wasn't something I often did then. Now it is a regular occurrence for no other reason than I love beautiful things in my home and I am worthy - isn't that reason enough?!

> Side note, do you ever just do things for yourself, just because? Not because you should, someone told you to, you felt you must, just because you wanted to. If you don't, it is a freeing experience to do so. I encourage you to try for yourself.

Special delivery: egg shipment day

Egg shipment day arrived and I locked in my sperm donor, the rest then happened pretty quickly. My eggies arrived unscathed and were fertilised. Remember when I told you I had ordered an eight-pack of eggs? Well nine arrived. How come you may ask? To be honest, I am not sure. Even the fertility clinic admin was surprised. I was not complaining, instead I chose to take it as a sign of good fortune. All nine were successfully thawed and fertilised, resulting in three embryos (Yippee!); two x seven cells and one x eight cell embryos. I had already begun my medication protocol, complemented by Omega-3, Calcium, and Vitamin D supplements. This was the first cycle I was intentional about how I spent my time.

For me, this meant choosing not to do acupuncture. I realised my reason for doing it was robotic and I didn't feel this time round I would benefit from it as much as I had previous cycles. Mainly I felt it would be a rush for me to get there on a regular basis and being in a stressful job already, I was very mindful not to add any more stress into my life. That decision felt freeing, and I knew it was the right one for me. I was already incorporating deep breathwork into my daily habit. I didn't need to 'do' more just because I thought I should when it didn't feel right to me. This was the start of me coming back to myself, although I didn't realise at the time.

The next step was to arrange my embryo transfer after a check of my hormone levels to determine the best date for transfer. The day was arranged and I booked a few days off work firstly to have the procedure, allow time for rest and implantation to begin and because I just wanted to. I knew right from the very beginning that for me to do this donor cycle I would book a few days off to just focus on what had happened and be with myself. Surely that wasn't too much to ask, was it? What I have come to realise about that cycle, actually, I think I knew during the cycle, was how disconnected from myself and the whole process I was. There were so many great things happening, sooner than expected and yet I wasn't excited. I was pleased, but it felt like a tick off the old IVF checklist.

I was the final appointment for the morning and had 1 x 8 cell embryo implanted (receiving a physical connection with my baby). Just as I was called in for my turn, the sun streamed through the clouds with such brightness and beauty. I felt lucky. I was blessed to have an 8-cell embryo implanted in the eighth month. *Surely this is a sign of good luck!*

I remember during the transfer my blood pressure dropped quite a lot and I wasn't sure if I was going to faint, vomit or both. Blessed with a support clinic and staff, I rested, drank some water and nibbled on a few lolly snakes. It took nearly forty-five minutes before I felt well enough to sit up and by then I felt knackered. I had had this happen before, both during egg collection and embryo transfer, so it was nothing new, just not nice. So after more rest, I headed home for a very quiet few days. I had prepared a few meals in advance to take care of myself during that time and by the next day what I felt were early pregnancy symptoms began to appear. Cramping, nausea, sore boobs, all of which continue to intensify over the next few days. I truly believed it was related to implantation, which was supported by medication I continued to take up until one week post transfer.

It wasn't until this time in my life, I began to allow people to offer help. I had finally reached a point where I didn't want to be a solo warrior anymore and began to wonder if maybe it wouldn't be so bad if I said yes instead of no when others made a gesture of help or support. *What's the worst that could happen, my ego gets bruised?* Not that I wanted that to happen but a shift was beginning inside me. One where I began to ponder what if... *Could there be another way for me to live my life?*

I had always seen myself as an independent woman and held that image with great pride. Now, there's nothing wrong with it, but I feel I took it to the extreme, where I wasn't open to receiving help from others. In fact, my consistency in saying no to any offer of help gradually led to fewer offers. Funnily enough, this affected me to., I saw it as people rejecting or abandoning me rather than me saying no all the time so they just stopped offering. This was how it typically went:

Them: "I know someone who might be able to help with X, would you like me to contact them for you?"

Them: "Can I grab you anything at the shops while I'm there?"
Me: "No thanks, I'm good, I've organised a click and collect later in the week?"
Them: "Do you need anything (when I was sick)?"
Me: "No thanks" I felt guilty asking for help when sick like I was being a burden
Them: "Can I help with your dating profile?"
Me: "No thanks, I've got it covered."

I was too embarrassed to ask for help let alone have someone read what I wrote. These people knew me, what would they think of me? I was much more comfortable allowing strangers to read my profile.

Them: "Can I help you with your resume?"
Me: "No thank you."
What if they didn't like what I wrote or worse, said it wasn't good enough?

The fear of being critiqued was too much to bear. I would much rather go it alone.

It was a matter of pride for me, that I could do it all on my own, as much as it was a way to keep myself at a distance without allowing anyone to get too close to me. I valued my independence highly and saw it as a key strength of mine, personally and professionally. It made me feel safe and in control. And being in control made me feel safe. In reality it was keeping me at a distance from the very things I wanted most - connection and belonging.

I remember a strange sensation one day during the two-week wait, where I was out for coffee with my family and felt like I was six months pregnant. I felt heavy, tired, nauseous, I had a metallic taste in my mouth and was out of breath. It was almost like an out of body experience. Strange huh? I must admit that I did take this as a sign I was pregnant. Then within a few days of me stopping the meds (about eight days into the two week wait) those same symptoms began to disappear. Trying not to panic and feel disappointed I had made the earlier decision to wait until my two-week wait blood test (and not test early). I had tested early before, and all it did for me was create a further sense of panic, which is the last thing any woman needs when trying to conceive. By the morning of the blood test I had begun to spot and my heart sank seeing drops of blood on my underwear. Deciding to remain positive until I knew either was for sure, I had my blood test and as I waited, I felt this sinking feeling in the pit of my stomach and pain in my heart. I knew Aunty Flo was on her way and I just felt sadness and disappointment. Actually more sadness than anything else. My brain was in overdrive again:

This egg was meant to be the magic fix. My eggs weren't good enough and a donor egg was meant to fix that. So why hasn't it? I'm never going to be a mum am I? I'm running out of time for more cycles.

I felt down and plain sad for most of the day until I heard from the nurse that the pregnancy blood test came back negative. It occurs to me how hard this call must be for the nurses who see so many women enter their clinic hopeful, to then hear those dreaded words, "Sorry, you are not pregnant this time".

Yes often we already know this to be the case, but the sting felt from hearing those words never eases no matter how many cycles you go through. It is heartbreaking, disappointing, frustrating and anger inducing all rolled into one each time. And the poor nurse tasked with delivering the news must feel awful too. Imagine ringing someone who is so desperately hoping for a miracle and you have to bear the news that will instantly shatter that dream into a million pieces? Yet they deliver such news with kindness and empathy each and every time (well they did for me anyway), which I greatly appreciated.

Sadly the first donor cycle went down and I failed. I know others would say to me, 'Dianne it wasn't a failure,' but that was exactly how I saw it. I felt numb, disappointed, frustrated, angry and sad. I could not fully comprehend what had happened. I felt disconnected from the entire process and what I was feeling after failing my first donor cycle only served to reinforce that very thought. *What was wrong with me? I wanted this to work so why wasn't I more connected to this cycle?*

Some interesting revelations came about the following days and thanks to my good friend who introduced me to tapping, I finally discovered why this was the case. There were plenty more tears. *Why didn't it work? What else could I have done? What shouldn't I have done?*

The circle of unhelpful and overwhelming thoughts began to quickly consume me again as it had previous cycles. It was not helpful at all, and quite powerful and destructive if allowed to take hold. I was extremely emotional and in shock and retreated inwards (as I often did when feeling overwhelmed). I limited my interactions and conversations with others, all the while yearning for someone to just make it okay. My dear friend Janine reached out and we scheduled more tapping sessions together.

At our first session after this cycle, I felt numb and really disconnected to self. Even connecting over Zoom, Janine noticed. We began tapping to see what came up. As I was tapping I repeated the statement: "I release my need to have a biological child using my own eggs. Pretty much straight away, I was overcome with emotion and the tears just gushed out. The tightness in my chest and lump in my throat were too hard to ignore and sobbing then took over. I was not ok.

Janine: "Can you tell me what you are thinking and feeling?"

I couldn't speak, instead uncontrollably sobbing, feeling embarrassed at doing so. I detest crying in front of others and feel a great sense of shame when I do. Like it's a weakness (which it isn't) and that I should be able to hold it altogether (which I shouldn't).

Me: "As soon as I started reciting that statement I felt a heaviness in my chest particularly across my heart, and that emotion travelling up my throat and out of my eyes, hence the tears. I felt like it just wouldn't stop, just very heavy and sad."

Janine: "That is an unprocessed emotion that has been sitting there, waiting for you to release it."

Me: "I thought I had processed moving on to using donor eggs, but I guess I haven't."

Janine: "Give yourself some grace, it's a big deal and it's ok to take as long as you need to make sure you are ok with the decision. No matter how long that takes."

Me: "I know, but I also feel a huge sense of urgency to make a decision and get on with it if that makes sense."

Janine: "I completely understand. How do you feel now?"

Me: "Surprisingly I feel a huge weight has lifted emotionally. I also feel clear headed now in terms of going down the donor

LETTING GO AND REDISCOVERING MY PATH

conception path."

Janine: *"That's great! Perhaps the tears were the final part of the release for you?"*

Me: *"I feel you could be right there. As I think about using donor eggs, I feel good about it. I have explored using my own eggs and it just isn't going to be my path to motherhood".*

We ended our session there and I knew I'd have a good nights' sleep. I was exhausted.

The dormant grief was released through the tears. That physical act provided such a huge emotional reset.

I am definitely not the type of person to share or show my grief with others, preferring instead to hold it in and keep it to myself. I think it's partly due to fear of how much will come out, and also not wanting to bother anyone else with my problems. This time, though, I did share my grief with Janine during our tapping session and discovered that despite me thinking that I had, I hadn't fully released the want to have a child using my own eggs. This was where the sobbing was coming from, and I could feel it deep in my chest and throat. Not that I felt going down the double donor path was wrong for me, I knew in my heart it was the right decision. I guess what I hadn't fully considered again (see how this has been a recurring theme throughout my life) was my emotional response to it all. I had to truly come to peace with a significant change in what I thought my life path would be.

So I allowed the sobbing to come out in all its glory without judgment or holding back. The physical release that came with it was amazing. I never realised how much emotional weight I had been holding onto and boy the difference I felt by letting it out. So much so, when the sobbing eased, I instantly felt lighter and I had come back to a place of peace. We continued tapping to invite harmony through my body and more positive energy surrounding my donor decision. This too felt empowering, loving and calming. My tapping statements included:

"Even though I never expected I would need IVF to have a baby, I thought I would meet a man, fall in love and have babies the traditional way, I deeply and completely love and accept myself."

Gone was the frantic energy surging through my body and numb headspace, replaced by a glowing warmth and relaxed shoulders and neck (this is usually where I hold my tension). I don't think I have ever slept better than I did that night and by the next morning I felt clear-headed and my mojo returned.

This was quite a defining moment for me, in the sense that this was the moment I fully embraced my choice for the double donor path. I felt the alignment throughout my body, heart and soul. This truly was the right decision for me and my future baby. Have you ever felt something was just right in all of your being? That was what this felt like for me. No second guessing myself, no doubt of any kind. It is the most calming and peaceful feeling I have ever known.

From that very moment I made a choice, the choice to surround myself with the energy of what I wanted to create (i.e. a loving and warm home for my baby, and becoming a mum to a child I carry myself). This last one was quite important to me. I wanted to experience the blessing of pregnancy, to watch, feel and notice my body change as she created a new life. Having now actually experienced this joy, it remains a true blessing for me, feeling so grateful for the experience and all that it taught me about myself, life, my family, my body and living my best and truest life. How did I do it? Far from being easy, it involved changing my thoughts, habits, behaviours and subsequently my actions. All one step at a time, and over the matter of a few short months, I began to notice the difference. Others did too.

August 2022, I met Tara through a business Facebook group and had collaborated on a multi business competition. During the course of which we became quite close and I loved her energy. I felt heard and seen and she became a source of guidance and strength for me during my IVF cycles when I was using my own eggs. She was running her own coaching business at the time, and I signed up for six weeks of 1:1 work with her. Our sessions were weekly and a deep dive into my emotional psyche. Unpacking thoughts, "How did I see myself?" "Where did this self-image originate?" and "How would I like to see myself?"

Each question brought tears and a heaviness in my chest. A suffocating heaviness. Our first session I remained fairly quiet, nervous at what was to come from our discussions. I felt conflicted between wanting to remove the stuck energy inside of me that was hindering my ability to become a mum, and at the same time filled with fear at what might be unearthed. She was gentle in her approach, not pushing too hard the first session together, telling me, "We'll ease in to our time together today, but I do want for you to get the most out of this time and I'll prod a little harder each week we are together not to cause harm but to aid release."

Me: "Ok, I must admit I am nervous at what might come out. I avoid my feelings at all costs, pushing them away and carrying on like everything is fine"

Tara: Why do you do that?"

Me: "It's pretty much a habit for me to do so, it's just what I have always done. I also feel like I don't want to burden others with things that don't really matter in the scheme of life anyway".

This pretty much described me to a tee: people pleaser and loner.

CHAPTER 5

Discovering SOSI and my truest self

"Knowing yourself is the beginning of all wisdom"

– ARISTOTLE

Now I know what you are probably thinking. Dianne, what on earth is SOSI and how does this relate to your story? Stick with me, and I promise all will be revealed and make perfect sense!

Back to the very beginning, it was December 2020 and I had hit my wall, crying endlessly, severe insomnia, feeling frustrated with life and completely overwhelmed.

I knew the reason why.

I had ignored myself, my needs and innermost desires for too long again and my body was ever so kindly telling me to STOP and take notice. Albeit not very politely. I knew things needed to change and just didn't know where to begin. It felt insurmountable and overwhelming if I am totally honest. It all felt too hard, and I just didn't have the energy or brain space for any more. I was in a job that was demanding more of me than I was capable of giving, it was a two-person job requiring support from a manager whose role had yet to be filled, nine months after the previous manager left.

At the time I did the best I could to hang on and help keep the ship afloat, but I was drowning and I could clearly see myself heading down a familiar path. Recovering from a breakdown (which I now term my breakthrough) was a long, hard slog and I didn't want to end up back to where I started. Hadn't I learnt anything? Perhaps not.

Randomly scrolling Facebook one night, mainly because my brain just couldn't function doing anything mindful at that moment. I came across an ad by an American lady named Tonya Leigh who was running a free week-long workshop titled 'The Week of Calm'. I truly believe in that moment and still to this day, this was a sign for me to take notice, which I did. I stalked her some more and discovered she ran the School of Self Image (SOSI). Calm was what I was deeply longing for, so I signed up and figured it couldn't hurt. I might even learn a thing or two. What I didn't know at the time was how deeply impactful that one decision would be towards my life over the next three years in particular. In reality, it still impacts me in extraordinary ways to this day. Have you ever made that one decision that has changed the trajectory of your entire life? Well this was mine.

The Week of Calm was due to start the following week so I scheduled it into my calendar and downloaded the workbook to have ready for my notes, thoughts and hopefully some inspiration to turn my life around. I wasn't asking for much surely! Now by the time the following week arrived, I was even more exhausted, experiencing greater brain fog and paralysing sadness and the urge to withdraw from my life and everyone I knew. This had come at the perfect time, it couldn't get any worse could it?

I remember crying my way through the entire week, each daily lesson hitting home harder each time, like it was directly speaking to me and only me. I kept that workbook, completing many more lessons with Tonya over the next three years, but this one stood out the most as it spoke directly to me. Everything she was talking about, I desired and was really struggling with. For any of you who haven't come across Tonya, she is a kind and soft spoken woman who epitomises elegance, charm, femininity, sass, courage and self assurance. She is actually so much more than that, but I'll leave you to come to your own conclusions about her.

The first class in particular was an aha moment for me, where Tonya discussed the choice between allowing versus resisting. In essence it asked, am I going to keep doing as I have always done and want for a different outcome, or am I prepared to surrender and be open to growing, learning and evolving no matter how uncomfortable it may be at times? I am proud to say that I chose the latter and have never looked back. How did I do so?

That in itself was quite the ride, taking one step forward and what felt like two, three or five steps back at times. Nonetheless, I was committed to taking that one step forward each and every day. Sure, my ego got bruised along the way, but that is part of the growing process. To separate ourselves from our ego and allow our mind and bodies to become more expansive, open, vulnerable and ultimately aligned. To grow I put myself in new surroundings with new people and new experiences. Yep, taking myself out of my comfort zone and building the muscle to be comfortable with feeling uncomfortable. I did this over and over, meeting some amazing people along the way who are now close friends, rediscovered my creativity in being in these new places, and shared my struggles with those further ahead of me.

YOU ARE WHO YOU SURROUND YOURSELF WITH

Think of your own life, do you do the same things with the same people at the same times? Do you want more? I invite you to think deeply on this and listen to what your heart (not your head) is telling you.

I believe the daily tears while watching the lessons were an opportunity for me to release so much emotional baggage that was pent up, so I could begin with a clean and emotional strong slate. I have to say that week was exhausting for me both physically and emotionally, but so bloody worth it. Kudos to that version of me who was brave enough to put her hat in the ring, even though she didn't have the energy, but showed up anyway. You go girl! I was introduced to the concept that our thoughts directly influence our feelings, and so if I wanted to feel better, I needed to have better thoughts. Surely it wasn't that easy!

It was a long road following that week, with a lot of emotional baggage to release and with each release new discoveries showed me more to heal.

I had never really paid much attention to my emotional health, generally only my physical health, so this was quite the eye-opener for me. I was always the kind of girl who just soldiered on, recklessly blind to how this habit or behaviour was detrimental to me. Am I alone here?

I think in part, it's due to generational beliefs we have probably all grown up with and a strong expectation within the wider community that we don't acknowledge nor explore our deeper feelings. Instead, we push them to one side and in the event we might struggle (as I clearly was) we keep ourselves busy in the naive hope it'll make it all better.

I never saw calm as a superpower and soon came to learn that that was exactly what it was and is. And I wanted a big slice of it please! No cream or ice cream needed. How was this even possible?

What soon stopped me in my tracks was something I had been avoiding my entire life and I was now being asked to face it head on. The need to resist and escape my emotions. I was an expert at it and a pretty darn good one too, even if I do say so myself. I was now being asked to face what I have so expertly avoided, something I did not want to do. I would later discover that by doing just that I would return home to myself, calmer, happier, more settled within myself and truly ready to live my desired life with open arms (and heart). So I showed up to each of the five lessons, assessed where I was at and how I wanted to feel. By the end of those five days I was physically and emotionally exhausted, I had never cried so much in my life.

I was so far away from feeling calm, and yet found comfort in what she had to say about checking in with our self image. This was something I had never even thought about let alone spent time actually doing. Such an aha moment!

Following that course, in January 2021, I decided to join her membership as an annual member. I gifted myself twelve months to see what I could do to transform my life and how I saw myself. Since joining I have found my way back home to myself. Don't get me wrong, it has been quite a ride, with many tears shed and tantrums thrown (all behind closed doors of course). In the beginning it felt like this was the sign I was looking for to lift me from my funk and help me get my life back on the trajectory I saw and wanted for myself. And in many ways it was, it was also a lot of soul searching and admitting to myself my part in relationship breakdowns, experiencing workplace bullying, being childless in my mid 40s, single and generally feeling dissatisfied with life. These were all my responsibility and choice. I say choice as I did little to not be in this position, when I had the power to do so. I just didn't see it at the time. My fear and lack mentality held me back from going after what I wanted.

It was and felt so easy to blame everyone and everything except for me. In reality I was the one who made all of the decisions (or not) which led to where I was then and now. That I have to say was quite a blow to my ego, which I might add I didn't realise was as high as it was at that time. It felt like a slap in the face that I was to blame for where I was and all that I felt I didn't have. It also stung in my heart and that's where it hit and hurt the most. I had created where I was and what I didn't want, based on fear, overwhelm and mindlessness. What I did find interesting during this revelation was I didn't wallow for too long, which I would have previously sat and stewed in the poor me mentality feeling sorry for myself and yet doing nothing about getting out of it. I was quite the professional at doing this. Are you too? There was always something so comfortable about doing so, yet I felt miserable which now as I sit writing this I realise how opposite that sounds. Funny how the mind works and mine unfortunately was in full control of what I did and thought without me taking any leading role. I allowed it to run rampant as it always had done and then wondered why it was acting like a confused and somewhat obnoxious child.

I cannot tell you how life changing it was to hear that I was in charge of my thoughts and directing my life (by thinking on purpose) and not just a product of social and genetic conditioning. *Like am I the only one who went holy heck, I can do this,* life isn't just pre-programmed for me?

Let's take a back step for a minute and I'll share with you how I reached a point where I believe SOSI and my three subsequent guides appeared for me. It was because I was ready and open to a new way of thinking, acting and being. Tara was my first guide, followed by Janine in August 2022. I truly believe as a collective force I moved closer to where I am now: faster, calmer and with more confidence than I could have without them. I always found it interesting where there have been certain times in my life where people have seemingly randomly come into my life and as I look back now, I realise there was always a reason for them doing so. In the case of Tonya, Tara and Janine, they entered my life to challenge my status quo, motivate and support me to think with care and intentionality. To help me reach my deep-seated fears and emotions tucked within my subconscious, and which were significantly blocking my path to motherhood (I believe).

Realising that I had a choice in my life, even more so I was in the driver's seat and could influence my path at any time. That it wasn't selfish to put myself first, and not in an arrogant way where I don't ever consider anyone else. More in a loving, selfless way, where I matter and am no longer cast aside so as not to upset or offend anyone else, and in doing so upset myself for always putting myself as the end of the line. I understand some of you may be reading and thinking to yourself what the hell was wrong with me? Why wouldn't I put myself first? I guess all I have to say to that is I didn't and didn't feel I should or could. I believed I was there to serve others and that their happiness was more important than my own. I also believed in the romantic space that a potential partner needs were more important than mine. Yes, I know I can hear you screaming, *Dianne seriously!* It was beyond empowering to hear other women say it was okay for me to have a voice, my own voice and if others didn't agree or stick around, that was okay too.

It was quite a journey I must say, chipping away at each of the many layers, with tears shed, revelations celebrated and all the while a growing sense of pride (for myself) and my connection with others. This was what I had always deeply craved. And all it took was me to open myself up to being vulnerable and holding space for myself.

REFLECTION

What do you think might happen if you open yourself up to the universe and she delivers? Now if this is a negative thought, consider switching the question to what would you like to happen?

Remove all distractions, put your phone on silent and quieten your mind.
Take a few deep belly breaths. The deeper the better.
What do you notice?
How do you feel?
What can you smell or hear?
How are you feeling in your body? Can you name it?
This is your future self connecting and talking with you.
Take some time to journal your feelings, insights, questions and thoughts.

JOINING SOSI

Joining the membership for a full year was incredible. I was challenging myself, practising new thoughts, habits and behaviours, as much as meeting new people and putting myself in new surroundings to inspire and build my creative muscle. At the end of the year I felt a huge weight had been lifted and I was on the right path. Each of the monthly topics were exactly what I needed at that time, and that continues to be the way for me to this day. I am proud to say I am still a SOSI member and can't imagine leaving this amazing community of women from all over the globe. So much so that I made some big decisions over the past couple of years, starting a tea business, trying for a baby using double donor conception, closing my tea business, writing my first book, and setting up my Youtube channel. The support, guidance, honesty and learning from these amazing women who are all in different stages of life across the globe is invaluable. This is the importance of a tribe, who you surround yourself with truly does matter. It can inspire, motivate and energise you or it can drain, stress and burden you - *it's your choice!*

I am finally at a place where I know who I am, what I want and believe with all my heart that I will get there.

✎ REFLECTION

I encourage you to consider what you truly want for your life and do you honestly believe you can get there? What answer do you come up with, and ponder why this answer presented itself to you.

Is it fear talking, your intuition, or what you think you should be doing/ being as opposed to your heart's desires.

If I can then anyone can, I invite you to take a moment here, pause and journal on that very thought.

What comes up for you?

CHAPTER 6

Donor Cycles

*"Be gentle with yourself.
You are doing the best you can"*

– PAULO COELHO

DONOR CYCLES

I naively assumed that donor cycles would be a breeze and not as time intensive as my previous cycles using my own eggs. I had totally forgotten about the counselling sessions I would again need to undergo, both in terms of donor counselling, donor egg counselling as well as genetic counselling before progressing any further. Both sessions were relatively uneventful, I had completed counselling sessions previously during my IVF cycles and so was prepared to be open, vulnerable and somewhat realistic about what was happening.

In terms of the donor counselling session, this involved sharing my previous report from my old clinic to have on my current file. I remember the lady I spoke with being quite friendly and gentle in her approach. I loved how she acknowledged my journey to date and honoured my resilience and knowledge of the process. I must say I was a little taken aback at first, no one had complimented me and I remember feeling quite strange receiving her praise. I brushed it off with some random comment and continued on with our discussion.

It later helped me to reflect back on my life and appreciate just how far I had come personally and all I had experienced and *'survived'*. She provided some practical ideas, such as creating a scrapbook for my future bub about my donor conception journey and information about the donors I would choose and why I did so. As well as adding my details and future bubs to the donor sibling registry should he or she might wish to make contact when they reached adulthood.

Side note: I knew right from the beginning that I would be open with my bubs about how they came into the world and save the donor profiles for when they were ready/ wanted to know more. I believe our self image and identities are hugely important and I never for one second wanted my bubs to ever feel less than, or that who they are was hidden from them. Now this was my choice and I respect others who choose an alternate way. Neither is right nor wrong, but being open with my little one about their history and genetics was the right choice for me.

The genetic counselling session was straightforward as I had already completed one with my previous clinic, so it was a matter of reviewing that report and ensuring the sperm donor I was choosing with my current clinic was compatible with my previous genetic testing. My next step was arranging my sperm donor order through the donor coordinator.

My final counselling session was in relation to using donor eggs, during which some interesting questions were posed to me:

Counsellor: "Would you plan for two children given you may have leftover embryos if you fall pregnant before using all three? And given your current age, how and when would you do so?"

Me: "Yes, I am hoping to have two children close together if I can. Ideally I would carry them but I am also open to a surrogate as well".

Counsellor: "Would you be open to sharing photos of my child with the fertility clinic to pass on to the egg donor?"

Me: "Yes I would, that would be such a lovely idea"

Counsellor: "Would you be open to your child meeting their egg donor?"

Me: "Yes, absolutely! I intend to be very open about my choice for donor conception and should any resulting child wish to reach out to their donor I am only too happy to support them to do so in any way I can".

These were questions I had thought deeply on for quite some time, but was thankful for the reminder to keep that front of mind as my decisions did not just impact my life but potentially my future child's. It was important to me and to them that I remember this.

As I mentioned earlier, after two donor cycles, I was blessed with my precious baby girl Eva. There is a lot of similarity between IVF cycles using your own eggs versus using donor eggs. Numerous blood tests, internal ultrasounds, medications to predict ovulation timing with relative certainty, in amongst angst, worry, stress, anticipation, hope and optimism. For me the main difference was the timing of it all. Seeing as I wasn't using my own eggs the lead-up part to embryo transfer felt less stressful as I only had to focus on one procedure instead of two.

Looking back on both cycles, I can clearly see how disconnected I was from both it and myself during the first cycle. Waiting to tick tasks off the list with little regard nor celebration for all that I accomplished or was blessed with along the way.

Cycle two however was the complete opposite to cycle one. Intentional, mindful, curious, present and focused were words that come to mind to describe that time. I'll let you in on a little secret as to why that was the case. Feeling crushed and at a complete loss why I didn't fall pregnant in the first donor cycle, I realised what needed to change and that became my why, and a big why at that.

I always believed my desire for motherhood was my why. In fact, my why was more about connecting to myself, prioritising what I needed and wanted, and living my life to the fullest with IVF featuring as a story within that, not the entire novel. Too often, I had been caught up in the tunnel vision of chasing my precious baby with blinkers on to the rest of my life and what was going on around me. That's not to say my desire to have a baby wasn't important and by no means am I devaluing anyone else's choices or values. For me it just came down to my putting my life on hold indefinitely to pursue motherhood. Doing so was to my detriment. What kind of example to my child would I be in allowing my health (physical, emotional and mental) suffer in the name of desire? Not being my truest and fullest self in the pursuit of an outcome, not opening myself up to a different path to my desired destination. How would my child see themselves then? What would they learn? That the pursuit of what we want most in life comes at the expense of our health and wellbeing and that is okay? That what we want is more important than what we need?

These revelations hit me pretty hard. My ego certainly felt a sting there. What I ate or didn't and when, what I did and where I went or or didn't was focused around my cycles only. It had left me feeling exhausted, miserable, alone and like I was continually failing myself. What kind of life would I be bringing this child into? It seemed to be one of despair, misery, frustration, anger, sadness and isolation. Certainly not the loving, nurturing and thriving environment I saw us living in.

I wanted to bring my baby into a calm, peaceful, intentional and loving world (our world) and what I was creating each day was very far removed from that. Things needed to change, and they needed to change quickly.

The donor egg process could not have gone more smoothly for me, and quicker than first anticipated and yet I felt empty and hollow.

Where had Dianne gone in all of this? Where was the carefree, happy, loving life woman?

The woman who loved to meet up with friends and chat and laugh for hours?

The woman who loved to travel and explore new places or revisit favourite destinations?

The woman who laughed so much her belly hurt and tears streamed down her face?

The woman who didn't take herself too seriously?

The woman who chose to live her life, not hide away at home?

This became my reality, all consumed by falling pregnant. I never considered what might happen or I would do if that was never realised. Some may say that was persistence and optimism. I thought so too for a while, but I believe it was more a matter of blind faith, letting life dictate my path for me.

> **TIP**
>
> If, like me, you have low blood pressure, I found both the egg collection and the embryo transfer process was really taxing on my body as my blood pressure almost always dropped. To the point where I thought I might pass out, followed by intense waves of nausea. What I discovered was, instead of lying flat for the procedures, I tilted the headrest down a little so my head was slightly lower than the rest of my body. No drop in blood pressure nor impending nausea. In fact I felt pretty good afterwards. All it took was me asking for what I needed.

After my first donor cycle, I was given a choice by my fertility specialist to go again straight away as I had another two embryos to use. This is a common practice in IVF and one I had embraced many times, repeating cycle after cycle with little thought on my physical, emotional or mental self. This time was different. I had a five-day trip booked with a friend to a wellness resort in the United States that I was very excited about. So in typical Dianne fashion I calculated the timeframe to see if I did another cycle straight away when the transfer date would fall and the resulting pregnancy blood test. This led me to a crossroads I wasn't expecting. I would have had plenty of time to do another cycle and have my pregnancy blood test all before travelling.

My issue became that I would be roughly five weeks pregnant by the time we flew and I was reluctant to carry a heavy bag, let alone feel anxious about any foods I ate while over there. I was feeling the stress of it all work its way through my body before anything had even begun. There were pros and cons to doing another cycle straight away and also in waiting until we returned from the US.

In terms of waiting, it would mean I would start another cycle in two months' time, which in the scheme of how long my IVF journey had been up until then, was no time at all. Yet this niggling voice kept tapping me on the shoulder saying, *"You shouldn't wait, you've already waited and look at all the problems you have now. Waiting may cost you a baby! You are getting old, your biological clock is ticking and there's not much time left".*

All really helpful thoughts wouldn't you say? (Not!).

As I have mentioned before, my fertility specialist and her nursing staff were nothing but supportive and nurturing to me. I felt absolutely no pressure from them to hurry up and do another cycle straight away. If only I could eliminate the stress I was putting on myself.

I must have spent nearly a week tossing back and forth between deciding to wait versus going ahead straightaway. What it boiled down to was I wanted to really enjoy my time away at the wellness resort without having to worry about anything. It was supposed to be a time to delight in facials, massages, good food and sightseeing. All without worry of lifting my bag, DVT or food poisoning (Yes I can be overdramatic at times). As I thought about it, it made sense to wait and honestly, it just felt the right thing to do. Give my body a break for a couple of months to detox from all the IVF medications, get back in sync with myself and have a fabulous time away (which I did). For the first time, I chose me first. To allow myself to be worry-free and just embrace the experience of travel and fun again (it had been quite awhile). And so I did.

Deciding to delay

As soon as I made the decision I knew it was 100% the right decision for me. As soon as I had made it and spoken with my specialist, I instantly felt a weight lift off me I hadn't even realised I was carrying. The timing of and the decision itself were absolutely what I needed and was meant to do. What resulted from those next few months was a lot of introspection about what I had been doing throughout my cycles and why. It all came down to me feeling that I should be doing them in order to fall pregnant and that Google was telling me they were the supposed guarantees of success. The question I never once asked myself was: Do I want to do them? And what benefit (if any) were they to me?

While I found acupuncture relaxing in the beginning and am so glad I did it back then, it became a stressor for me in terms of time availability and cost (defeating the purpose of relaxation). It did help me in more ways than relaxation; it taught me to connect with my body and helped to regulate my pulse to be much stronger by the time I finished going.

Going 100% gluten and dairy free initially felt amazing in my body, but I wondered if I was going overboard. I say that as now and then I do eat some cheese or bread that contains gluten, and I feel fine. What I discovered was that I could eat both dairy and gluten in small quantities while predominantly remaining gluten and dairy free. In fact, eating calcium rather than relying on calcium tablets was probably better for my body anyway. Rather than denying myself foods like chocolate, biscuits, or ice cream, could I create a version that supports my body while also acknowledging my cravings? I am human like everyone else after all.

That then left me with my mindset about IVF, pregnancy and motherhood in terms of what I truly believed was meant for me. Funny thing was, all throughout my cycles I never for once truly doubted my ability to make my desire a reality. Sure, there were fear-based moments when I questioned when it would happen and what I needed to do to make it happen, but I never felt I was not destined to become a mum. *Have you ever had that feeling of inner knowing, you can't quite describe it but it sits deep within your heart and soul and you know it is meant for you?*

Even when those around me advised me to stop and be at peace with trying without success. Even when the odds were against me age wise. Even when my history to date had told me I couldn't.

In spite of all that, I chose to continue on, chose to do so in my late forties and well aware of the potential risks involved. I chose to be a single mum and learn to rely more on and trust myself more than ever before.

During my two months off I chose to spend that time reprioritising me, eating what my body needed, moving when it needed to and spending more time with friends and family. I could feel the old Dianne returning, albeit an updated version of her.

I felt lighter in my body, my skin, hair and eyes looked clearer and I had more energy. The stress, anxiety and all-consuming thoughts had really taken their toll on me the past few years and it wasn't until I stopped that I realised this.

Late November 2022 I commenced my second donor cycle, full of optimism, love for self and stripped away from anything that was no longer serving me. I felt prepared this time round and connected to the process. As usual my cycle involved blood tests and medication protocols. This time though I spoke up regarding my wishes, sharing my experiences with previous cycles with my fertility specialist, where I felt implantation cramps and a number of other pregnancy symptoms but as soon as I stopped taking progesterone (usually day five within the two week wait), the symptoms disappeared within a matter of days and aunt Flo came. She asked me what I was looking for, to which I replied, "I think it could be low progesterone having an impact".

That wouldn't be too far a stretch given my age at that time (47), and at the very least couldn't we test it to check? Tears began to roll down my eyes as she said to me, *"Dianne, I am the IVF expert. You are your body's expert. Let's make you a baby."*

Finally I felt heard! Beyond elated was how I felt in that moment and noticed that I had a pep in my step for days afterward. I decided to not do a round of acupuncture for this cycle, I would eat based on what my body needed and kept my supplements range to a minimum. So when the time came for embryo implantation, we did a blood test prior to test my progesterone levels and I awaited the results, expected later that same day. To my relief (validating what I was already thinking) my progesterone was a little low (not critical) and so I was prescribed Crinone gel to begin the very next morning. Calling into the pharmacy on the way in to work, I excitedly collected my Crinone. I felt validated and also more than a little annoyed that I hadn't asked earlier in my IVF journey. Thoughts such as 'I could have been a mum already,' were swirling around my brain. Luckily I caught them and focused instead on congratulating myself for pushing through my fear of asking for what I want and hoping this meant my precious embryo would stick.

I noticed within about four days of starting the Crinone how much my energy levels increased and the exhausting fatigue disappeared. Clearly my body was desperate for the progesterone she was lacking. To be honest, I was so surprised at the difference in my physical and mental wellbeing.

I realised that it's ok to ask for what I need. What that taught me was by asking for what I wanted I was sitting within my aligned and authentic self. And that my fertility specialist was the one for me, because she was open to hearing me and testing my levels. Now I wasn't extremely low, but low enough that progesterone support was needed and I immediately felt the difference.

The two-week wait felt like one of the longest, because there was so much relying on this cycle. I was putting immense pressure on myself, no one else. I felt the cramping, nausea, fatigue, sore boobs as I had in previous cycles. This time I didn't assume it meant I was pregnant, but I tried to remain lightly optimistic. Now usually I would receive a phone call from the nursing staff in the early afternoon. On this particular day that didn't happen.

I admit I did feel nervous and the pangs of control returned.

Expecting a call between one and four in the afternoon, I felt a little anxious by three o'clock and rang the nursing staff.

Me: "Hi, it's Dianne, I am expecting blood test results today following my cycle. Are they in yet please?"

Nurse: "Hi Dianne, yes we are expecting your test results today. As soon as they come in we will call you ok?"

Me: "OK, it's a little unusual to not have heard yet."

Nurse: "Yes I understand the lab is running a little behind but we will definitely have your results today."

Me: "Ok thank you".

I was still feeling uneasy, like maybe something was wrong, so I tried to keep myself busy at work until the phone call came. I finished work just after four o'clock and still hadn't received a phone call.

What is going on? In all of my IVF cycles I have always had a call by now.

Thoughts raced through my mind.

Maybe there's nothing to worry about and it's good news that's coming? Maybe it's bad news and no one wants to tell me? Why don't they just call already?

What is taking so long? What do I have to wait for? Just tell me already!

I rang the nurse again at six o'clock.

Nurse: "Hi Dianne, I know it's hard but please be patient, we will call you tonight."

Me: "Ok thank you".

I was not in the slightest patient at all. *What the heck is going on?*

I tried to keep myself busy (and distracted) making dinner, walking my pup Lady and having a shower. Once this was done, though my mind wandered back to waiting for THE CALL.

How long is this going to take, the suspense is killing me!

I was so tempted to call again but also felt guilty and slightly concerned the nurse would be cross with me for constantly following up. *She did say she would call.* And yet as time passed my anxiety levels increased. Negative thoughts swirled around my head. Expecting the news to be bad all the while hoping for a miracle that this time I would receive the news I have so longed hoped for. *Could it be tonight?*

Eight o'clock came around and still no news, I knew the nurses clocked off at nine o'clock and was slowly resigning myself to not knowing my results today. *Perhaps tomorrow was meant to be that day and I was better off just accepting that and getting some much needed sleep? Who was I kidding!*

Eighth thirty rolled around and I decided to call one last time for the night.

Nurse: "Hi Dianne, I'm so sorry we still don't have results, the lab is running behind for us today. I will call you though as soon as I hear anything, ok?"

Me: "Ok thanks."

I admit I was feeling quite deflated by now so I took myself off to bed, wondering what tomorrow would bring. Would it be the news I am hoping for? I lay in bed staring at the ceiling, my brain buzzing and feeling wide awake. I had the strong feeling I wasn't going to get much sleep tonight.

Was this a lesson from the universe teaching me faith and patience? It certainly felt that way.

By 9pm I was still wide awake, thinking perhaps I was meant to get my results the following day. Maybe that was meant to be. This was going to be a restless night!

I remember the phone call as if it were yesterday. At 9.18pm, as promised, my nurse rang me with the magic three words I wanted to hear: "You are pregnant". That made me happy but what made my heart sing and tears flow was hearing my HCG, oestrogen and progesterone were super high. These were the magic numbers I wanted to hear. I burst into tears over the phone. I really was pregnant and not just a little, but a lot!

Nurse: "Hi Dianne, sorry to call so late but I know you have been anxiously waiting for your results so I wanted to call you back tonight."

Me: "Thank you so much, I really appreciate you doing that. I know you have clocked off for the night."

Nurse: "Absolutely no problem at all. You know what I am going to say don't you?"

(Now while Aunt Flow had not visited me I was nervous that all might not be as I desperately hoped for. This had happened previously and I didn't want to get my hopes up, while at the same time conflicted as I did want to hope. I felt conflicted, hopeful and just wanted to know the answer tonight.

Me: "Umm, I am hoping it's good news for me?"

Nurse: "Well, I am very pleased to tell you that you are pregnant."

Me: "Oh my goodness that is great news".

Nurse: "Congratulations, your HCG is 200 U/L, your progesterone is 2000 U/L and your oestrogen is 1880 pg/ml".

At this point I burst into tears, I had never received hormone numbers this high. I asked my poor nurse to repeat the numbers as I couldn't read my own handwriting. I thanked her for calling me out of hours and after hanging up danced around my kitchen filled with elation and pride.

There was definitely no good night's sleep, and I was more than ok. I was pregnant!

That night was a very restless one, and I woke the next morning feeling tired and excited. I was just so proud of myself, as I rubbed my belly.

My precious angel, I cannot wait to meet you.

CHAPTER 7

Pregnancy

"A baby is something you carry inside you for nine months, in your arms for three years, and in your heart until the day you die"

– MARY MASON

I AM PREGNANT! I literally wanted to scream it at the top of my lungs. All the while a hesitation buzzed in my belly. I had been pregnant before and miscarried, experienced multiple chemical pregnancies and while part of me was hugely excited, another part much deeper down inside was scared, very scared history might repeat itself. Would it be that cruel again? I knew this was part of the IVF journey, and perhaps the most unpleasant one for me, anyway.

How do I balance the sheer excitement as I should be and want to be, with honouring my deepest fears, all without letting them take over and derail me?

In amongst all of these feelings I also felt a pang of guilt that I couldn't use my own eggs to fall and stay pregnant. I was scared of what others might think of me and my decision. *Would they judge, criticise or ostracise me?*

Luckily my pregnancy was relatively easy. Easy in the sense that I experienced mild nausea but nowhere near the morning sickness I had heard from others. Pregnancy fatigue is a whole different ball game, though. Trimester one I was okay, by trimester two and certainly during trimester three I felt the full weight of fatigue hit me. I guess I never truly realised how much of a toll it took on a woman's body carrying and growing a precious human. Here's where my wonder woman complex comes in. I have always seen myself as superhuman, believing there was nothing I couldn't physically do nor overcome. And yet I was tired, needing a nap every day after walking the dog. By no means is this a complaint, more self realisation of how my life was changing before my very eyes.

Am not sure about you and your pregnancy experience, but for me I had a couple of milestones firmly cemented in my head that meant I had reached a safe zone. The first being achieving twelve weeks pregnant. The reason for this was that I had miscarried before that milestone and as we all too often know the first twelve weeks are when miscarriages can often occur (not to say they can't happen past this time). That dreaded 'M' word filled me with fear and dread, and I so desperately wanted to make sure it didn't happen. I get it may sound silly, but reaching twelve weeks was so incredibly important to me, and when I did, some of that fear and dread melted away (not completely though).

It felt like forever to reach twelve weeks (bearing in mind the way IVF works is that when I found out I was pregnant I was already six weeks along by then). Wracked with anxiety and nerves about what could go wrong, I cheered when I hit twelve weeks.
I MADE IT!
Funnily enough I was still racked with nerves and fear. I guess it was a little naive of me to think they would go completely.

Although I still didn't feel *'safe'* in my pregnancy although by this stage I did announce to close family and friends my joyous news. What I mean by safe was I didn't feel one hundred per cent confident all was and would be ok, meaning I would deliver my precious baby at full term. It's interesting how we want something so deeply and yet are so scared by it at the same time. Do you ever feel this way? And it wasn't a paralysing type of fear, but it was quite prominent and niggled away at me for almost my entire pregnancy. I began to wonder if in fact this was normal, especially with recurrent

IVF failure. What I do know is that it felt uncomfortable, as I learnt how to become comfortable with the uncomfortable (if we ever truly can, that is).

The next milestone was to reach twenty weeks. Again, in my head and heart I felt if I could make it, I was safe and could stop worrying (is that even possible?). By this stage, I had also begun to see my fabulous obstetrician, Dr Harry, who I must say took the best care of me and often relieved my worries with his calm demeanour and proactive approach to my care.

Trimester 1 (conception to 12 weeks):

I think I was around ten weeks pregnant when I first met Dr Harry. My GP had recommended him as they were well known to one another and my GP felt he would be the best obstetrician for me. The reason being was my age and that my pregnancy was the result of donor IVF. Dr Harry is a lovely man, so personable right from the get-go. I felt confident he would be the best OB-GYN for me and I was excited for the road ahead we would travel together.

I remained on the Crinone gel (Progesterone - via a vaginal applicator) until I was around twelve weeks pregnant just to make sure bubs was ok, plus to give my pregnancy the best chance of success. Given I was in my mid forties, my progesterone levels were low so the additional boost would not only support my overall wellbeing but also aid in preparing the lining of my uterus to receive the embryo, have it implant and stick. And by stick, I mean, falling and staying pregnant. Crinone gel is widely used in IVF as progesterone support is essential for getting and staying pregnant after fertility treatment. This was even more important given this was a donor conceived baby where my ovaries need the extra support in the very early stages. Generally, this would be up until twelve weeks pregnant. By then my body would be producing enough progesterone because of the pregnancy, I would no longer need extra supplementation.

I admit that I was a little nervous to stop taking it, it was more fear-based than anything else. My blood tests showed my oestrogen and progesterone levels were super high, as to be expected during pregnancy so there was no medical need for me to continue taking Crinone. Funny how fear can often take hold of us at times and attempt to derail our thoughts. Despite all of that I admit I was nervous to stop, worried something might happen to my precious girl. I trusted Dr Harry, and decided to trust in my body and all she was doing for me now, and weaned off the Crinone gel. Despite my initial fears, nothing happened, I had no side effects and my energy levels still felt good. I had my first blood test to determine the baby's gender. I absolutely wanted to know what I was having, more so to plan what I would buy for the nursery. I wasn't bothered whether it was a boy or girl, so long as they were healthy that's what mattered most to me.

At fourteen weeks pregnant Dr Harry rang me with my blood test results.

Dr Harry: "Good morning Dianne, I have your baby gender test results, would you like me to share them with you?"

Me: "How exciting, yes please Dr Harry!"

I was bursting with excitement. I couldn't wait to hear what I was having. Boy or girl didn't matter, but knowing the gender made them even more real. I just couldn't wait to hold them in my arms and kiss them all over. Another step to motherhood becoming a reality for me.

Dr Harry: "Well I am very happy to say you are having a girl".
Me: "Oh that is great news!"

I proceeded to burst into tears. My heart felt like it was going to burst, I was having a baby girl. I felt a mix of pride, joy, love, anticipation and impatience all mixed together.

Dr Harry: "I will see you soon for your scan ok. Congratulations again".
Me: "Thanks so much Dr Harry, see you soon."

As we ended our call I jumped from my seat at home and fist pumped the air, dancing down my corridor with the biggest grin on my face. Lady did look at me like 'what the heck is wrong with you?' but nonetheless followed me around, her tail wagging with happiness too.

I AM HAVING A LITTLE GIRL! How am I going to focus on work now with such exciting news?

I can tell you that the remainder of the day I was very distracted, daydreaming about my precious little girl.

What would she look like?
Would she look like me?
What would her little personality be like?

I imagined her ten little fingers and ten toes, her tiny nose. I imagined smelling her, seeing her. It was becoming real!

I already knew her name, and had done since I began my

IVF journey, many years ago. Her name was a connection to her ancestors and some very special people in my life. Had she been a boy, I also knew his name and like hers, his was a connection to his ancestors and some very special people in my life. Those special people are my maternal and paternal grandparents. Throughout all of my IVF cycles I had always felt the strong presence of my grandparents, especially my grandmothers and couldn't have imagined any other name for my precious darling.

It wasn't much longer before I saw my precious girl for the first time. I had my scan in Dr Harry's office the week after receiving news I was expecting a girl, and felt tears stream down my face. There she was in all her glory, a beautifully perfect developing mass. Filled with pride and love for my precious bundle, I had done it. I really was pregnant, she was real and all was going smoothly. What more could I ask for (aside from getting rid of those pesky fears and anxieties).

After a fairly smooth first trimester I was taken by surprise when trimester 2 came around. I noticed I began to rub my belly, and then catch myself when others were around as I hadn't shared my news yet. While there was no bump yet, I felt my baby in me; it really is the most unusual feeling. I say unusual as I know there is no movement to feel, and yet I could feel her. It was just so beautiful. Maybe it was a sense of her I was feeling, whatever it was it was magical and beautiful all rolled into one. I am eternally grateful I didn't experience extreme morning sickness, I mean call me a wussbag, but for me the worst thing is feeling nauseous. Like, just let me throw up already! I know I'll feel better then. But to just feel nauseous and then nothing happen would have to be one of the worst feelings for me.

I discovered gluten free party pies and sausage rolls as the saviour to my never-ending nausea, especially first thing in the morning. I don't know what it was about them, but they were literally the only thing that eased my nausea. To the point that I would eat through two to three packets a week. They were also delicious which helped too. In fact I ate them so regularly that my Labrador Lady knew the packet and sat right near the oven until they were cooked in the hopes that she might get a taste of the pastry.

Trimester 2 (13 to 27 weeks):

Reading my old journal entries from my IVF cycles brought back sweet memories of joy, excitement, anticipation and fear. Reminiscing about the waves of nausea, resolved by gluten free party pies and sausage rolls (who knew they could help so easily!). Horrified, I remember mentioning the pies and sausage rolls to Dr Harry that I was eating them for breakfast as it was the only food that didn't make me feel ill. In my head it seemed quite odd to be eating them for breakfast, and yet here I was doing so pretty much everyday from about fourteen weeks pregnant to nearly twenty weeks when the nausea began to ease. I can still taste their deliciousness and the smell as they came out of the oven was just intoxicating.

Dr Harry laughed and said "Whatever you need to do to ease the nausea". I was stunned, like it wasn't that I hadn't tried ginger nuts, ginger tea and the like. But literally nothing apart from this delicious savoury yumminess worked. And so I continued my weekly purchase, sometimes twice weekly.

I remember my other odd food that my body was not only craving but also seemed to work against nausea was gluten free chicken nuggets and chips (also sometimes for breakfast). Now I think about it, my body craved carbs first thing in the morning and nothing else I ate seemed to ease the second trimester nausea. Thankfully I was never actually sick.

At twenty-two weeks pregnant and again at twenty-six weeks pregnant I had the glucose test for gestational diabetes. This is a standard test during pregnancy, although it is usually only conducted once. The reason I had it twice was that Dr Harry was extra precautious with my pregnancy and wanted to get on top of things should anything arise (which it didn't from this test). The test itself isn't particularly exciting but it is quite disgusting to taste. It is a glucose drink designed to detect diabetes in pregnancy by checking how well my body regulates blood sugar levels. Gestational diabetes is a common pregnancy complication, thought to affect one in ten pregnant women. A series of three blood tests are taken one hour apart. The first blood test is taken on an empty stomach to check blood sugar level baseline, followed by drinking the glucose drink. No eating or drinking then for the next two hours. Blood test two taken one hour after taking the drink, with the final blood test two hours after taking the drink.

It reminded me of a super sweet lemonade and cola mix,

so sickly sweet. Thankfully I did bring a bottle of water and a sandwich with me to have once I had finished the test. Not only was I hungry, but also nauseous from not being able to eat or drink beforehand.

This was the trimester when the fatigue well and truly hit me like a tonne of bricks. I had read about the effects of pregnancy fatigue during trimester two but honestly wasn't expecting it to be so fierce for me. Even walking the dog, which had never been tough going for me before, saw me wanting to rest when we got home. Clearly, I hadn't thought through the toll on my body in growing a little human. I noticed a little bump appear, although this could have easily been mistaken for me eating a big bowl of pasta. At a random visit with my GP, his nurse was horrified to hear him describe me as looking bloated. Lucky for him he and I have known each other a long time and I laughed at his comment. I should mention at this point that I didn't actually start really showing, like noticeably showing until I was around seven months along.

Trimester 3 (28 to 40 weeks):

After the second trimester had thrown me around I was so looking forward to my last trimester being a breeze. No I know I can hear you laughing. I honestly thought I was over the worst of it and would just sit back and bask in the glow of motherhood. One thing I will say was my skin, eyes and hair were positively glowing during my blessed pregnancy. So many people commented, and I even noticed. What I struggled with was extreme fatigue, sciatica pain along my back and hip and the return of my dreaded nausea. Now it wasn't all bad, although there were days I felt like it was. I guess that is pregnancy in a nutshell, isn't it?

What I will say is my confidence in seeing my baby girl earthside outweighed my fear of something going wrong. I constantly rubbed my belly, talking to my baby girl and feeling her movement increase as I focused on deep breathing and reconnecting with myself. Her movements seemed to mimic the speed and pace of mine. My present self at the time didn't know this was key to shaping the happy, calm and cheery girl I rock to sleep each night.

Throughout this trimester I wished that I looked pregnant and yet didn't. I looked more like I had eaten a good pasta meal, not grown a precious human. In total I put on 8 kilograms, knowing full well my little bundle would be a tiny one at full term. And on one hand I was grateful for a small weight gain, but there is just something about a woman who looks undeniably pregnant, and I wanted that for myself. I looked like I had eaten a big bowl of pasta. It was around 8 months pregnant I began to show and did so proudly for those few weeks before I held my precious girl in my arms.

I did purchase a few pieces of maternity wear, more so that it was nursing friendly and also enabled me to show off my slight bump with pride. There is just so much out there on the market, I found it easy to be sucked in and want to buy everything. I realised I didn't really need it, while also gracing myself with the permission to purchase a few items. I loved the pieces I bought and wear them, even now I still do.

Getting close to delivery day, I knew it would be a planned caesarean at 38 weeks pregnant and I could have a support person with me in the delivery room. Who would I choose? That question did bring up some fear, worry and inadequacy in me. *What if no one wanted to be in there with me? Could I really do this alone?* I didn't have a lot of confidence in myself at that point if I am honest. Rising to the surface were my people pleasing and fear of being judged, and they weren't taking any prisoners. What to do?

CHAPTER 8

Birth and Early Motherhood

"Birthing is the most profound initiation to spirituality a woman can have"

— ROBIN LIM

The time was almost upon me. My precious baby girl was soon to be earthside, like for real no longer a dream but soon to be a reality. I knew very early on I would be having her via c-section at 38 weeks pregnant to ensure no risk to her or me. While I had been looking forward to the experience of giving birth (Yep you heard me right), I was also well aware of how much of a risk my age played in all of this and wasn't about to be so close to the finish line of becoming a mum to risk it all at the end. Yes I would have liked the experience of a vaginal birth, but it wasn't to be and I was ok with that. My priority first and foremost was me and my baby girl.

My ob-gyn and I had also discussed very early on that I was looking to commence my maternity leave at 36 weeks pregnant. I remember thinking at the time that was a possible scenario and had a conversation with work about my intended leave start date, albeit with confirmation to be made closer to the time. I naively thought I would be ok to work up until having my baby girl and wouldn't need or want any extra time beforehand - rookie error, I know! By the time I hit 30 weeks I was counting down until my leave began at 36 weeks. While I hadn't put on much weight I felt exhausted, nauseous and a little anxious about the C-section. What I was most nervous about was the epidural; the thought of having a needle in my spine sent shivers down my spine, literally!

I was truly blessed with a supportive manager and team throughout my pregnancy which made it all the easier to navigate. My age did influence my fatigue as I was what I now know to have been in the perimenopausal stage of my life. Fatigue and digestive issues were just a few symptoms of this, not really aiding my pregnant body being it's best and energetic self at that time. While I felt young at heart at 49, my body was feeling less so. It was time to recognise I wasn't a kid anymore and could no longer carry on with little regard for my body's need for rest, relaxation and calm. That was the first eye opener to being an older mum and what my life would look like once bubs was born.

I knew that I wanted support for myself in the operating theatre. This was a big deal after all and it was finally dawning on me how major an operation this was going to be. How would my body and headspace cope? I also wanted someone to share this momentous experience with, and be my photographer and cheerleader. As someone who has spent most of their life quite independent and not seeking the help of others, this was a new sensation to feel and one I actively embraced.

I knew I wanted to have bubs in my local private hospital. It was a new maternity ward and I'd heard great stories from other mums about their experiences. Bonus it was also less than a ten minute drive from home. I booked in for a free tour, my mum coming along with me and I fell in love with it. An instant feeling of belonging and this was the place for me. This was definitely where I wanted to become a mum, no doubt about it. Hospital admission forms were completed online and I was all booked to go.

Now to get ready! There were a few tasks to organise which I hadn't given much thought to until now. Who knew there was so much to do to have a baby!

I had decided that I wanted to take a full year's maternity leave to spend with my baby. Afterall I have spent years working to have her, and I wanted to soak it all up without the rush of having to return to work. I was in a position financially that I could do so and knew this would be a big transition for me. For the first time in my life I chose to put myself first and give myself the time I needed and wanted. I was also very lucky that my employer was supportive and approved my leave request.

There were a couple of things left for me to finalise before commencing my leave:
- Who do I want as my support person? I was blessed with many options, but I knew deep in my heart there was one person I wanted by my side. My sister, I couldn't imagine anything more special to share with her. Yes we had our differences over the years but she was who I wanted to be by my side - would she be happy to do so?

I thought about when to ask her and what I wanted to say. I know I can be clumsy in how I speak from my heart at times and wanted to be really intentional with my words. I felt a face to face conversation was best, and organised for us to meet together over lunch and hope she would say yes. It was probably one of the first times I spoke from the heart to her about why I wanted her, while also understanding if this wasn't something she felt comfortable doing. She said yes! Woo-hoo! I was beyond stoked when she told me she would be happy to be my support person. And it certainly helped to calm my nerves over the C-section process.

- Packing my hospital bag. I don't know about how others may have felt, but I was so excited to do this, and researched what to include. I must have packed and repacked it four or five times. This activity represented the reality I was soon about to delight in, the arrival of my baby girl. When I was packing for me, I was also packing for her, the time was imminent for her arrival. I reminisced over what I wore in the hospital when I was born, yes, my mum had kept some of those precious outfits, and now I was getting to pack them for my baby girl to wear. I remember a close friend telling me that she bought herself a couple of new pyjamas to take to the hospital as a gift. What a loving idea! I found some beautiful pieces at Jasmine and Wills that I could personalise (which I did), as a memento of the day I became a mum. I understood others thought of this as frivolous, which they were perfectly entitled to. For me, this moment was years in the making and I wanted to celebrate and not just while in hospital but each time I wore them, as a reminder of what I had achieved. Yes, I had achieved this.

Now 38 weeks pregnant, with mine and bubs bags packed I headed into hospital in the wee hours of the morning accompanied by my sister. I could feel the anxious and excited energy between her, Mum, Dad and I at what was soon to come. Our lives were all about to change forever, in the best possible way. I was about to become a mum! What I didn't know at the time, was that this would trigger the deep connection and sense of belonging I had desired my entire life.

We arrived at the hospital and headed up to the maternity ward to get all checked in and settled into my assigned private room. Now, even though it was a matter of hours before I held my baby girl in my arms I did as I would always do when first arriving somewhere I am staying overnight. I unpacked my bag and set out my medications on the bedside table and hung up my clothes. Well, when I mean clothes, I mean spare pyjamas and my dressing gown, along with my toiletries. Nothing like being prepared hey!

As I look back on that time, I think it was a way for me to focus my nervous energy and calm myself as best I could. I couldn't wait to meet my baby girl, and at the same time was dreading the epidural procedure. I freely admit I am a total wuss when it comes to needles and this was no exception. I find that quite ironic given my choice to do multiple IVF cycles all of which involved numerous injections, surgeries and injection protocols. Nonetheless I never got that comfortable with needles, and I must admit, we are still not on super friendly terms today.

Birth time

Here I am, unpacked and ready to go. We meet the nurse, who runs us both through what will happen in theatre and performs the standard blood pressure & heart rate checks. Compression stockings applied (to help prevent blood clots and deep vein thrombosis) I am wheeled out into the theatre waiting room. We meet another lovely nurse who runs through the same checks again, tests my memory to make sure I know who I am and what procedure I am in the hospital for. My sister was given her 'scrubs' to put on, which she was particularly impressed with. The shirt had some great pockets for mobile phones, pens and all sorts of things which we both felt would be totally practical in the non-hospital world. Sadly, she had to return them, but one can hope can't they? My last piece of attire to wear was my hairnet and I was dressed ready to go...

I went into the operating theatre on my own initially to have the epidural, and then afterwards my sister would be brought in. I remember the theatre being absolutely freezing cold. I am not sure if it actually was that cold, although some of the nursing staff did comment it was a bit chilly in the room that day, but I was literally shaking. I suppose it didn't help that all I was wearing was a hospital gown that had now been undone at the back, so here I was sitting on the side of the bed, my back area exposed, hunched over and hugging a cushion. Apparently, the hugging pose helps to separate the vertebrae in your spine for ease and accuracy of the anaesthetic injection prior to the epidural being inserted. I just wanted that part over and done with.

Trying not to shiver, mainly because I didn't want the injection to end up somewhere it shouldn't, I focused on the music playing in the theatre. As I entered the room, I could hear the mumbling of voices behind me, I turned briefly and could see some nurses and my doctors talking. I could hear jazz in the background.

Doctor 1: "Now, what music do we feel like today? This jazz is going to send me to sleep!"

Nurse: "How about some Bollywood, that'll keep you awake?"

Doctor 1: "I was thinking of rap music."
The nurse giggled.
Doctor 2: "No gangsters in here."
Nurse: "How about some classical?"
Doctor 1: "Oh gosh, not that crap"
They all laughed.
Doctor 1: "Ok let's play some instrumental music then."

I tried not to laugh. I knew I was supposed to sit very still, especially given I was going to receive a needle in my spine soon, but I couldn't help but laugh at their banter. It did ease my nerves though.

I remember the sting of the first injection containing the anaesthetic to numb the area before having the epidural. The sting wasn't as painful as I had imagined, although it still hurt and I remember the doctors telling me they were going to lay me down on the bed ready for the procedure pretty quickly before the epidural took hold. I didn't think it would act so quickly, given I have never had one before and just felt it couldn't possibly numb so quickly. Boy, was I surprised!

I kid you not, by the time they laid me down on the bed and straightened me up I couldn't feel anything from my waist down (which is what's meant to happen - phew!). Finally, my sister was by my side and the blue screen was lifted up in front of me. I had chosen not to watch the procedure, mainly because I just didn't want to. I was happy for the doctors to do their thing; they are the experts after all and then show me my little girl once she was out. I have always had a phobia about seeing my own blood, I am totally fine with anyone else's except for my own. If I do see it, my blood pressure drops straight away and I pass out, not ideal when having surgery, so I decided to pass on watching and just wait for my baby girl to be handed over to me.

My doctor spoke to me during the entire procedure as did my anaesthetist, telling me what was happening then and next, as well as checking in on me. I found it comforting and reassuring, that I had chosen the best team to have around me. My sister also kept close tabs on me, sitting right beside me so I could call out to her when feeling lightheaded or nauseous, which I did a few times. My team was extremely responsive to my needs and finally, the time had arrived when my baby girl was coming out. The best way I can describe it was that I was a pinball machine, being tugged left and right as they moved my baby girl down and out of me. You see she had dropped into position when I was 36 weeks pregnant and then literally the night before she arrived I felt her move back up again. Now I am sure the doctor didn't believe me when I told him, reassuring me she couldn't possibly have, and yet even he had to admit that indeed she had and he had a bit of trouble getting her out. Perhaps she was quite comfy and not ready to come out yet?

I can't tell you how much medication I ended up taking for the dizziness and nausea but it was at least two to three rounds as my blood pressure kept dropping. I don't know if you have ever experienced it, but it is truly a horrible feeling and one I didn't need in the middle of surgery. The time had finally arrived! She was here. I still watch the video my sister kindly recorded of the moment the blue screen was pulled down for me to see her, in her all glorious mess, umbilical cord still attached. She was just perfect! I shed a tear at that very moment, and my heart swelled up like it was about to burst. I waited to hear those first cries, for me that meant she was breathing and ok. I didn't hear them initially and felt a pang of panic. *Is my precious girl ok?*

I could see the nurse off to my side cleaning her down and removing some gunk from her nose and mouth, then came those sweet first cries. Yep, another few tears were shed and relief swept over me. She was here. She was just beautiful. She was ok.... Talk about an overwhelm of emotion in that moment, it was just the most perfect day of my life.

I turned and watched as the nurse took her over to weigh and measure her, my sister just beaming with love and pride for her niece. I could see them talking but couldn't hear too well what they were saying. It seemed the nurse was telling my sister what she was doing as she was doing it. I could see them looking at one another a lot and my sister nodding and smiling. My sister later shared with me the exchange:

Sister: "The nurse was lovely. As she washed Eva, measured her and cleaned her mouth and nose, she was telling me everything that she was doing. She was very open and considerate of my presence. She even asked me if I wanted to cut the umbilical cord, which of course, I said yes to. It was harder to cut than I thought, like a piece of rubber. I totally thought it would be softer to cut."

I didn't think she could possibly beam anymore, especially with the nurse asking her if she wanted to cut the umbilical cord.

It felt longer than it probably was, until I finally held my baby girl in my arms for the very first time. Wrapped in a blanket she was just perfect. Our first cuddle and picture together - my heart simply burst with love and pride. It was the most beautiful picture of Eva, my sister and I. My dream of motherhood had now become a reality!

All that was left now was to stitch me up and reunite me with my daughter in our room. Well, so I thought anyway. What ended up happening was quite the opposite and nothing that I had planned for. Remember me mentioning earlier about the room feeling really cold, well Eva was taken up to the NICU as her temperature was quite low. I didn't think anything of it at first as it was cold there and figured she wouldn't be there long. Here's where what I thought would happen over the next 24 hours differs from what actually did happen. I figured she'd warm up in the humidicrib for a bit while I was sorted out then we'd reunite in our room and our new life together would begin. Umm that was not to be the case, not for 24 hours anyway.

As the doctors began the process of stitching me up, my blood pressure dropped and more medication was administered. I was feeling quite worn out by this stage. I think a combination of an early start, a restless night's sleep, and my body requiring a lot of medication to keep my blood pressure stable. That wouldn't hit me until later that night. I remember laying back, closing my eyes and just soaking in what I had just done. I had my precious baby girl, the one I was told I was too old to have and should give up trying to have. It seemed quite a lot of time had passed before I was told they were finished and I would now make my way out to recovery. As I was wheeled along to recovery I think

I had a nap, exhausted and and looking forward to cuddling with Eva.

The one thing I love about hospitals is the warm blankets; there is just something so comforting about them and I love the added weight on my body. Coming out of surgery, your temperature naturally drops so I was blessed with a couple of warm blankets along with what I can only describe as a warm air bed placed on top of me. That's what it reminded me of. A large inflatable contraption with a hose at the end blowing warm air in to keep me warm. I am blessed with my body being fairly quick to recover and perk itself back up again, this time though it took awhile for the anaesthetic to wear off so I remained in recovery for much longer than expected. Not having had this type of procedure before, I didn't know how quick it would take to regain feeling in my body and I wasn't particularly worried; those blankets kept me toasty warm.

I did eventually make it out of recovery and up to the NICU where I saw Eva in a humidicrib, fast asleep and looking very comfy. The nurse informed me that Eva's body temperature was a little on the low side still, nothing to be worried about and she would remain with them until she saw the paediatrician. I sat up in my bed and just stared at her, fast asleep in all her perfection and beauty. I couldn't wait to hold and nurse her. So I was wheeled back up to my room, my sister accompanying me and we took in what had just happened with joy and pride. I was starving by this stage as I hadn't been allowed to eat since 7pm the night before (so no breakfast), and I was keen to eat something, knowing if I didn't, nausea would soon come back to visit me, and I wanted to avoid that at all costs.

Not long after thinking about how hungry I was, a nurse came with some snacks to tide me over until lunch, which was about an hour away. My sister kindly completed my daily meal preferences for me, while I munched on my snacks. Bearing in mind this was about 11am and we had been at the hospital since 6am. Sadly, visiting hours were almost over, so I would have to wait until the afternoon visiting hours to see my parents and share with them my delight in becoming a mum and them as first time grandparents. The plan had been that I would have Eva by 9am, then back up to my room by 10.30am so they could visit with me. Life had other plans, and instead gave my sister and I some time together which was awesome.

So I slept and ate lunch, then dozed a little more. I'm not sure how long I slept for, but I remember being awoken by a nurse and the paediatrician who informed me that Eva would remain in her humidicrib in the NICU for 24 hours just as a precaution. Her body temperature was rising fine and there were no other concerns, but as she was a low birth weight (2.47kg) they wanted to give her the best start. I would now have to wait till the next morning to hold my baby girl. I remember feeling incredibly sad and angry at life for blessing me with her, then keeping her away from me. What I would later learn was that this was a blessing in disguise, and the best thing for both of us.

Feeling a little lost, I rested as much as I could and was grateful for mum and dad visiting that afternoon. I did wish my little girl were with me, but knew she was in the best place for her. What I do remember worrying about was whether not having our first 24 hours together for skin on skin contact would negatively impact our ability to bond. I remember reading up on the benefits of skin contact following birth and was scared at not being able to give this to my little girl. In reality, I had nothing to worry about, we are as tight as ever, with that first 24 hours having no negative impact at all on our bond.

Visiting hours finished, Mum and Dad headed home and I was on my own in my room, not yet able to get out of bed. I underestimated how much rest I would need post-surgery so took the opportunity to get some. Not that I got a lot, in fact that first night was a rough one for me. Bouts of vomiting, low blood pressure and then by midnight, needing to have an ECG to check all was ok. This did little to give me the restful night's sleep I thought and was hoping to have. Still nothing that couldn't be healed and by the next morning, while feeling weary I felt better in myself. Once again, I was eternally grateful for the most amazing and supportive ob-gyn.

By the next morning, I could get up and have a shower. That was music to my ears! Slow and steady my body adjusted to moving again and the hot shower was just heaven on my weary body. Inhaling the steam to clear my congestion I felt a new woman in fresh pyjamas and settled into breakfast. Not long after my precious girl arrived, we were finally reunited. As the nurse wheeled her in I couldn't help but grin from ear to ear, my perfect little bundle was back with her mum, right where she belonged.

Our first snuggle was better than I could have ever dreamed of. I know there is a lot of research promoting the benefits of skin-to-skin contact for babies, but it has all the same benefits for Mum - I believe it does anyway. Feeling her tiny little fingers resting on my chest as she dozed off to sleep was pure heaven. I am eternally grateful for having those few hours just her and I until visiting hours commenced. Something I will treasure forever and never forget. She was so tiny and yet so incredibly precious. Ten long fingers and ten long toes all wrapped up in her blanket with her name embroidered, a beautiful gift from my cousin.

I am so glad I decided to go down the private hospital route, I cannot fault the care and attention the doctors, nursing and cleaning staff gave Eva and I during our stay. Nothing was a bother, and for me as a first-time mum, their advice and support were invaluable. In fact I remember one morning, around 6am when the night shift nurse came to do her final check on me before finishing her shift. She asked me why I hadn't called for her during the night, telling me she missed Eva and I. I was mindful not to take up too much of the nursing staff time unless I needed to as there were lots of other new mums on the ward at the same time as me and I knew I could hear a few babies that were struggling at night. Eva was a dream right from the beginning, even from those first few days she was sleeping every couple of hours and only grizzled when hungry. Apart from that she loved skin to skin time, cuddles and being snuggled.

My five-night stay in hospital was the perfect time to bond and allow reality to sink in that I was now a mum to this perfect little human. Taking Eva home felt really scary and exhilarating all at once. I loved having the nursing staff so close by and the sense of security it gave me. At the same time, I couldn't wait to bring Eva home to meet Lady and settle her to sleep in the same bassinet I had used as a bub. One that was made by my dad's hand, so it was special to share that with her.

I remember how tiny she looked in her rompers in the bassinet. She was such a precious bundle indeed. I was one thousand per cent wrapped up in the newborn bubble and loved every minute of it.

The sleepless nights were a huge challenge for me and one I don't think I could have prepared myself for before having a child. If you are anything like me, a lack of sleep directly influences my emotions. When overtired I can become quite teary, irritable, easily frustrated and short with those around me. In those very early days of motherhood that was very much me. Now I don't want to paint a picture of being ungrateful or that it was all bad because I'm not, and it wasn't. What I do believe in though, is speaking honestly and authentically about the reality of my experiences, knowing we each live our own journey.

Along with sleep my other challenge was breastfeeding. It was my choice to breastfeed from the get-go and I tried my best until Eva was about seven weeks old. My milk flow didn't fill her up; later, it became quite watery, with little of the creamy hind milk flowing. This seemed to give Eva terrible tummy aches that expressing and line feeding just couldn't fix for her. At the time I felt guilty and that I was failing her, which of course I wasn't. I was blessed with such huge support from the nurses and later a lactation consultant connected to the hospital.

At the end of the day I wanted what was best for Eva, and that seemed to be exclusively formula fed. I believe that with me trying to express, line feeding and regular breast massage, along with avoiding eating foods that may trigger her tummy upset, I was in the best headspace to decide. I did feel broader pressure many of us mums feel to breastfeed, although I must admit my family were incredibly supportive of me and also wanted what was best for Eva.

Now it was still a transition process to stop breastfeeding, and it was probably only a week or two after switching to formula that Eva's tummy issues ceased.

Speaking of support, another discovery I made was the extra love and attention Lady would need from me. This was also a huge routine and life change for her. Loving my baby girl as much as I do, I felt I owed her that much. This little person who was now in her space and family was no small matter to ignore.

I remember one particular early morning where I'd been up most of the night and by the morning burst into tears at an innocent comment by my folks. I was up very early for Eva's first feed of the day, at 4am, which had followed many restless nights navigating four-hourly feeds and then expressing my breast milk to increase my supply. I felt exhausted beyond words. My body felt emotionally heavy, my head pounded and eyes stung.

As Mum and Dad greeted Eva and I, the conversation flowed:

Parents: "How did you both go overnight?"

Me: "We were feeding every four hours and I had some trouble getting much milk when expressing"

Parents: "As long as she is feeding and settled, that's all that matters. You are doing a good job, it's not easy in the early days"

Me: "I am just so tired, I feel like a walking zombie"

Parents: "Welcome to motherhood! How about we take Eva upstairs with us and you grab a few hours of sleep?"

Me: "That would be awesome, thank you".

I then burst into tears, I knew motherhood would be sleepless nights, overwhelming love for such a precious being. What I never fully realised until in the throes of it, was how much the sleep deprivation would affect me emotionally. It clouded my judgement and how I saw myself. I felt like I was failing.

In the grips of exhaustion and somewhat overwhelm I just needed someone to comfort and reassure me as I did with Eva. And that's exactly what I received from them. The kind offer to mind my precious girl so I could sleep. Boy, what a difference a restful sleep made for me physically, emotionally and mentally. I literally felt like a new woman, clear-headed, emotionally strong and confident to be back in the world.

Another saving grace for me was arranging for the delivery of postpartum meals for my first five weeks at home with Eva. I had come across 'Meals for Mummas' at a Pregnancy and Baby Expo here in Sydney and tried one of their delicious, sweet treats. As many of us do, I held onto their flyer and gave it some more thought as it wasn't going to be cheap, but for me it came down to an investment in myself. As a solo mum by choice and one who knew she was having a C-section, I felt the investment was more than worth it. I knew that my body always healed well and quickly, but this was something new, and I wanted to give myself the grace of time to heal and bond with my little girl and not have to worry about food shopping or cooking.

I wasn't disappointed, the food was amazing and so delicious! Exactly what I needed in terms of wholesome nourishment for breakfast, lunch and dinner. Looking back I am so proud of that version of me who said, "Dianne, you are worth this, this service is available for a reason, use it!"

It made my life so easy, with no decisions about what to eat, and no need to grocery shop or cook. Just time to focus on healing, bonding, adjusting to motherhood and everything in between.

If you have the opportunity to do so, I strongly encourage you to take it. The financial cost, if you can afford it, is more than worth it in terms of time, energy, brain power and self care.

One of the many things I have loved about Eva coming into my life is watching her with my dad. Suffice to say, he is just as besotted with her as she is with him. They have become quite the sparring duo, it's quite entertaining to watch. Right from the first meet and greet when she was just one day old, it was love at first sight for him. She looked so tiny in his arms back then, so fragile, precious and beautiful. Not much has changed I must say, except she is not so tiny anymore. The same can be said for my sister and Mum, who are equally as besotted, and Eva is so blessed to be surrounded by so much love for her. It's exactly what I wanted for her.

I remember delighting in a close relationship with both sets of grandparents and I always wanted my child or children to enjoy the same. There is nothing quite like the relationship between grandchild and grandparent, and now I get to watch this unfold right before my very eyes. The cheeky smile as Eva coughs when Dad does, the grin she gives Mum when she hears her sneeze and the snuggles she gives to her aunty Jane when she's tired. It's so beautiful to watch and what I believe has contributed to Eva's calm, confident and cheery nature despite sleep regressions and teething.

Reflecting on how I was in terms of my thoughts, behaviours and habits during pregnancy, I felt calm, centred and at peace (in between the bouts of nausea), and I believe this also contributed heavily to Eva's calm nature. It was such an interesting and important lesson for me to learn about the impacts of our thoughts and actions on our bodies and energy. Something I must admit I hadn't ever thought about until meeting Tara, Janine and Catreeana and boy did they influence me in such positive ways.

Do you ever stop and think about why your life is the way that it is?

Are you happy with the way your life is? If not, what would you like it to be?

From my personal experience my life drastically changed and elevated when I ceased getting in my own way, connected deeply with myself and aligned my thoughts and actions with my desires. Sounds simple, doesn't it, and it really is. The effort that comes in is the implementing after you make the decision. From there it's one foot in front of the other, taking steps each day towards that which you desire. Focusing on your why, and tuning in to your internal guidance system to help you on your path.

I'm often asked if I would do this all over again if I knew then what I know now. This is an interesting and quite complex question. On the surface the answer may be, I would have started IVF earlier or gone down the donor route earlier. But at the end of the day, my response to the question is fundamentally no, as that might mean I wouldn't have Eva and I wouldn't be without her. I firmly believe I am exactly where I am meant to be and am loving life as a mum at 50. I know that I needed time to explore the donor route and process within myself, and let go of my want for a biological child.

In saying that Eva is my child, and I feel we share similar mannerisms and expressions, which others have often commented on. I do think that during pregnancy while she wasn't conceived using my egg, my genetics were mixed in. We each have our own individual fertility paths which are deeply personal, and for me, while I would love to have had Eva at an earlier age, I believe that she came to me when she was meant to. Yes, we were destined to be together, a bit cheesy I know, but it fills my heart just thinking about it.

What I'd say to my younger self

The advice that I would give to my younger self is to stand up for herself and to not feel scared to do so. Others' responses are not her responsibility, case in point remaining firm to request a blood test to check progesterone levels at the time of transfer, as well as articulating her desire to exhaust all avenues to use her own eggs in the first instance before moving onto donor conception. And most importantly that she did the best she could with what she knew at the time, and that is good enough. I think that too often we are critically harsh on our past selves and berate them for not doing, thinking or choosing better. We do what we do with what we know and understand at that time. Hindsight is a great thing. What if we chose to see the past as our teacher and reflect on the lessons learnt and where to go from there from a loving and nurturing space instead? Can you feel how powerful that sounds?

Motherhood today

I'm not afraid to admit I found the sleep regressions particularly challenging. As I have mentioned earlier, sleep for my emotional wellbeing is huge and I can literally feel the impact within a matter of days if I have less than a good few nights' sleep. Many say the four month sleep regression is the worst, I guess in part because it's one of the first and for a new mum this can be particularly challenging.

Is it just me, or did you find yourself not napping as much when bubs slept the older they got? I remember chatting with a close girlfriend who had come to visit one day and she mentioned this to me. It was such an eye-opener, I remember prioritising naps when Eva was really young and being advised to do so by what felt like everyone I came across. As she got older (above six months), I noticed I felt guilty for doing so, and often prioritised household chores during her nap times. In reality they could have waited and would have been completed when I was more refreshed and clearer headed. It's funny how guilt plays such an influential part of motherhood and as I am discovering, it never really ends. There is always something to feel guilty about, and we as mothers often put this pressure on ourselves unnecessarily.

We certainly wouldn't put anyone else under such intense pressure, why do we feel it's ok to do to ourselves? We are human after all and no one is perfect. Life is full of ups and downs and everything in between. What if we prioritise our own wellbeing, whatever that may look like on any given day. What might that look like for you?

As someone who has lived their life fairly structured, motherhood has blessed me with the desire to rethink my daily plans amongst teething, sleep regression, playtime and family meals. All for the better too, I might add. Yes there are always things to do, but I wonder, do they have to all be done right now, today, this week? The answer might in part be yes, but it also might be that it can wait until later in the day, the next day or week. Would that be so bad? What matters most to me is that there's enough food for both of us, clean clothing and bedding, toys and books to explore and a clean floor - Eva has recently started crawling. Having a black labrador who sheds a lot of hair, a quick sweep day and night is also a must.

During the six-week checkup, I spoke with my OB-GYN about my menstrual cycle not yet returning. I understood this was perfectly normal in breastfeeding mums, although I had ceased breastfeeding Eva by that stage. He wasn't too concerned but we did plan for some follow up blood tests in another two months time just to make sure there was nothing further needed. Aunt Flo never arrived so after having yet another blood test I was surprised to be told I was now in menopause. My oestrogen and progesterone were incredibly low, a known marker for the onset of menopause. Aunt Flo would never return, and I was about to embark on another life transition in and amongst early motherhood.

These early days were a little confusing as I wasn't sure whether my fatigue was down to being a new mum or menopause, same for my digestive issues and brain fog. Sure I had the odd hot flush every now and then, but it is uncertain where the line of menopause starts and ends. I do believe that being both a new mum and experiencing the onset of menopause compounded common symptoms and I am now in the process of learning new ways of thinking, being and doing that work for Eva, Lady and I. I feel like menopause and motherhood are topics not often discussed together and perhaps aren't relevant for many, but they are for me. Surely I am not alone here?

How could I best support my body as she changes, while also being present for Eva?

Am I needing to learn about myself all over again and this time round, I am starting with a clean slate?

So many thoughts swirling around my head, with no clear answers or direction in sight. Was I worried? No. A little uneasy, yes, but this time I trusted myself that I could navigate my way through safely, lovingly and calmly. A new path to explore, new insights to gather and new lessons to learn. Who did I want to become? What energy did she embody and what could I do today to take one step closer to her?

My dreams for Eva are for her to become a well rounded, confident, articulate, kind, compassionate and graceful woman. Someone who knows and trusts in herself deeply and is confident to set boundaries with herself and others. Who is kind in her heart and voice and appreciates the everyday, mundane and little things around her. Notice I mentioned nothing about career, education, money etc. Yes, I would love her to be in a career that she loves and is passionate about, with a good, solid education behind her, but what I want most for Eva is for her to have a strong and loving sense of self. One that is a solid foundation for her, and unlike me, not questioning her worth. Not in an arrogant way, but self-assured and loved. My hope for her is to never question her value or place in this world; to have her own back and surround herself with like-minded souls who grow, inspire and elevate one another.

Motherhood is an ever-evolving life lesson, and one that I feel so incredibly blessed to be experiencing with my precious girl. In the ten months Eva has been earthside, I feel like I have learnt so much already about her, myself, life, what I want for us moving forward, and my career path. Having worked in the corporate world since 2012, and in a variety of private and local government sector positions, my identity used to be heavily tied up in my career. That was who I saw myself as, a great and hard worker. Not that there was anything wrong with that, but I didn't see myself as anything but a great hard worker. That was until I had my breakthrough in 2017, and again now as a first-time mum. What I value and is most important to me has changed.

Yes, the security of corporate life is great and certainly provided me with a lot of security while pregnant and on maternity leave. What I crave most now is freedom, ease, and flexibility, not having to return to work full-time when my Eva is still so young. I saw work as an important part of myself and one that I felt made me a good mum, but I also wanted to balance that with time with Eva and not rushing around on the weekends.

Ideally for me three to four days work a week I believed would be a good balance. But what job would offer this to me and still provide us with a good income to travel every few years, support Eva with a good education and enjoy the odd meal out? A question I never pondered before and even while pregnant didn't think I would be considering. Ah how life has a way of changing you when you least expect it.

When I began my transformation from my 'breakdown' all those years ago, I was broken, feeling unworthy, never enough, and allowing others to make decisions about my life because I couldn't and didn't feel I made the right ones. I was living my life robotically and watching each day pass, with disappointment at not achieving or having all that I so deeply desired. By the time I discovered the world of personal development, I was almost at my rock bottom. Yet there was something inside me calling out to be heard, healed and loved. So with one foot in front of the other I walked through the fields of self-hate, pity, victimhood, overwhelm and fear. I scaled the walls of shame, self-loathing, people pleasing, disconnectedness and disassociation. I cried, hid away, comfort ate, didn't eat, cried some more and as each layer began to peel away, those negative feelings and habits were replaced with self-love, compassion, kindness, grace and self-care. It is and always will be a work in progress, life is never a full circle. We are constantly evolving if we choose to (which I do), and what we find further down the path is that it gets easier both to recognise, acknowledge and feel.

I now see myself as a woman who has her own back, is comfortable with feeling uncomfortable, knows it isn't selfish to take exquisite care of herself, and most importantly is a woman who truly loves herself. Now I never ever thought I would say that about myself, but it is true. I am perfectly imperfect and completely ok with that.

Motherhood has tested me in ways I couldn't have possibly imagined and I believe that is a part of the motherhood journey, lifelong. Becoming a mum has helped me open up my vulnerable side and ask for help, something I never used to do, as well as become more compassionate towards others, irrespective of whether I have walked in their shoes or not.

Life isn't always black and white, so our thoughts and behaviours shouldn't be either. So, without further ado, here are some of my top lessons in motherhood.

> *"Motherhood is a choice you make everyday, to put someone else's happiness and well-being ahead of your own, to teach the hard lessons, to do the right thing even when you're not sure what the right thing is ... and to forgive yourself, over and over again, for doing everything wrong."*
>
> – DONNA BALL,
> AT HOME ON LADYBUG FARM

My top lessons in motherhood

1. I don't have to be perfect.
2. There really is no rule book for parenting.
3. Each child develops at their own pace; it's not a race nor a status symbol.
4. My tribe accepts me and my messiness as it is. They offer help and support not judgement and criticism.
5. Life is not a race to be won but savoured and delighted in the everyday and mundane.
6. I know what is best for my daughter.

7. I am doing my best every day and that is enough.
8. It's ok to ask for help, and it does not make me less of a mother for doing so.
9. Contact naps aren't spoiling my child or ruining her for daycare.
10. Being a mum can be hard at times and at the same time a wonderful blessing and gift.
11. Sleep regressions do pass.
12. Expensive and numerous toys cannot replace love, attention, affection and fun together.
13. I don't have to know it all.
14. I am the best mum for Eva.
15. I am so incredibly proud of myself for persevering with my desire to become a mum. What an amazing model I am for Eva.

I hope you find some time in your day, make a cuppa and sit down to connect with your heart and what life, motherhood etc has taught you. Have you taken note of any lessons and made little tweaks? If so, I'd love to hear about them. Let's connect on socials or via email.

Thank you so much for taking the time to read about my journey and story. My wish is that it inspires you to go after what you desire for your life without fear, procrastination or self-criticism.

Love Dianne

EXERCISE

What are your dreams, hopes, desires for your little one/s or even for yourself? Have you taken a few moments to sit with this and reflect deeply?

Acknowledgements

To my parents and sister, and my closest friends — your belief carried me through the hardest days, your words held me up when I felt I might fall, and your presence reminded me I was never alone.

To my mentors, Tonya Leigh, Tara, Janine and Catreena — thank you for helping me find my way back to myself. In the moments when I felt lost in doubt or disconnected from my voice, you gently reminded me of who I am and what I carry. Your wisdom, encouragement, and quiet belief in me lit the path when I couldn't see it for myself. This story is more than words on a page — it's a reflection of the journey back to my true self, a journey you walked beside me with patience and grace. I will always be grateful.

To those who stood beside me through the winding, emotional, and often uncertain path of my IVF journey — thank you. This story, and this chapter of my life, would not

ACKNOWLEDGEMENTS

exist without your love, patience, and unwavering support.

To the medical team who treated not just my body, but my heart — thank you for your care, your empathy, and your dedication.

And to anyone reading this who is walking their own IVF or personal development journey: I see you, I honour your strength, and I hope this story helps you feel a little less alone.

Recommended Resources

There are a few resources I found particularly helpful during both my IVF journey, pregnancy and personal development. I hope they might bless you with the same love and care they gave to me.

IVF Journal = I used this for each of my cycles and love reading back through my experiences, thoughts, memories and challenges to see just how far I have come. My journal was from Write to me (www.writetome.com.au)

School of Self Image (SOSI) - Tonya's weekly podcasts are the insightful kick up the bum we often need. I highly recommend checking her out and see for yourself! Search School of Self Image wherever you listen to your podcast.

Monique Cormack is a holistic fertility care guru (I believe), having travelled down the IVF path herself. Aside from being just the loveliest human, she is full of practical tips and no nonsense ways to optimise male and female fertility. Her e books are jam packed with helpful advice and easy to follow meal plans. You can find her at www.moniquecormack.com

Glossary

D&C	Dilation and Curettage
EPU	Egg Pick up
FS	Fertility Specialist
FSH	Follicle Stimulating Hormone
GP	General Practitioner
ICSI	Intracytoplasmic Sperm Injection
IUI	Intrauterine Insemination
IVF	In Vitro Fertilisation
OPU	Oocyte Pickup
PMS	Premenstrual Symptoms
VARTA	Victorian Assisted Reproductive Authority

References

Endometriosis Australia (2012). Retrieved October 2024, from https://endometriosisaustralia.org/about-us-endometriosis-australia/

Energetics Institute (2005). Retrieved July 2024 from https://www.energeticsinstitute.com.au/what-is-core-energetics/

Everyday Health (n.d.) https://www.everydayhealth.com/wellness/eft-tapping/guide/

Fertility First (n.d.). https://fertilityfirst.com.au

Genea Fertility (1986). https://www.genea.com.au

Your IVF Success (2021). Retrieved February 2024 from https://yourivfsuccess.com.au/

Victorian Assisted Reproductive Authority (n.d.) https://www.varta.org.au

Victorian Assisted Reproductive Authority (n.d.) *Most women overestimate their chance of IVF success.* https://libraryguides.vu.edu.au/apa-referencing/7Webpages

Author Biography

Dianne Kelly is 50 years young and Mum to one-year-old Eva and six-year-old Lady. A corporate professional who is passionate about personal development and wellbeing. Her expertise is in breakthrough recovery. When not writing, you'll find Dianne in the garden playing with her kids, delighting in a good crime series and catching up with friends.

www.doubledonormuminmenopause.com

www.ingramcontent.com/pod-product-compliance
Lightning Source LLC
Chambersburg PA
CBHW020524080526
44583CB00013B/725